Shacking Up

40 Reasons Why NOT To
(Wise advice from someone who has)

By

Anne James-Sieff

ISBN: 1-4140-2861-X (Paperback)
ISBN: 1-4140-2860-1 (Dust Jacket)

Library of Congress Control Number: 2003099679

This book is printed on acid free paper.

Printed in the United States of America
Bloomington, IN

1stBooks - rev. 03/08/04

This book is dedicated to my three sons
David, Jacob, and Isaiah.

You were my light when my life was at its darkest.
I love you; you're the best.

TABLE OF CONTENTS

ACKNOWLEDGMENTS

I want to thank those very important people who encouraged me in my endeavor to get this book published. I want to thank Dennis Prager, who believed this message was an important one and gave me exposure through his radio show. You have changed the course of my life in a profound way, and I am forever indebted to you.

I would like to especially thank Dr. Laura Schlessinger. With her help we'll be able to reach millions more. I would also like to thank Michelle Anton for her swift responses and her patience.

Next, I want to thank Haley, my neighbor and my friend. She was there at the inception of this book. I would give her different chapters to read while we were driving to work together and get her input. She thought this was such an urgent message for people living this kind of lifestyle. Her comments to me were, "Anne, I want to learn from other people's mistakes so I won't make them myself and feel the pain I see them going through." You're to be admired for your moral stand, Haley. You're the best! By the way, she was only 18 at the time.

I want to thank Carina for correcting the first draft and for her insightful feedback. You're such a wonderful wife, mother, and friend. I'm so happy for the wonderful things that have happened to you. Your new baby, finding your birth mother, and having a great mother as well. Thank you for sharing in the thrill while this was unfolding. Wasn't it exciting?

I would also like to thank my editor, Stephanee Killen at Integrative Ink, for doing a beautiful job editing my manuscript. I also want to thank Akram Ibrahim, my Account Manager for putting up with me. You're awesome!

I want to thank my boys for their unconditional love and for being a beautiful example of what human beings should strive to become. Thank you for loving me regardless of how I was living at the time.

FOREWORD

Dr. Laura Schlessinger

I can't believe this book has to be written. It makes me sad to see women and men voluntarily, enthusiastically, even arrogantly pushing away a tradition of loving, spiritual commitment to degrade themselves and each other.

Look, I've given the facts out many times on my radio program to a caller either planning to or already "shacking up": shacking up promises an *increase* in "domestic" violence, anxiety, depression, infidelity, child abuse and molestation, children having emotional, social and academic problems, mental illness, and sexual acting out; shacking up promises a *decrease* in relationship quality, and stability, and sexual satisfaction, and a doubling of the rate of breaking up—especially if there is a subsequent marriage.

I've had callers to my radio program respond to this ugly list with, "That's your opinion!" When I remind them that these are statistical *facts*, they generally shoot back with, "Well, I'm different." I tell them that everyone believes that and I ask how they are indeed so different as to be immune to reality? Then…there is silence.

Of course there is the age-old "It's just a piece of paper" argument. It's just too easy to eliminate that one with, "Then why do you run with fear away from it?" Then…there is silence.

At this point, the call usually begins for real. Callers tell me of their messed up parents (affairs, violence, multiple marriages or shack-ups); their pain from abortions, promiscuity, multiple personal relationship losses, hurts, and failures (making poor choices in their desperation to feel some sense of connection they didn't get from their own families); their loneliness and purposelessness (even a connection with God has been lost); their total immersion in modern culture (where judgments of right and wrong have been suspended and immorality is apparently rewarded and morality derided, and immediate gratification is lauded).

Of course, there is no guarantee that following traditional values will always protect from hurt and provide peace and happiness—but, there is certainly a greater chance. Why? Because when people intentionally commit to each other in front of friends, family, and God, they are making a statement and a promise different from that of shacking up. Shacking up is about *measuring each moment* and determining if it is satisfactory to "me." Commitment is about measuring ourselves and determining if we are satisfactory to the "we."

Human beings become desolate when they feel or believe that life, and their lives in particular have no meaning. "What is the point of this/me, anyway,?" is the plaintive cry of depression. How can human beings avoid such depression? Certainly by putting meaning into their lives. How do human beings put meaning into their lives? By elevating their activities by imbuing them with honor, honesty, sacrifice, loyalty, courage, fidelity, commitment, and the gift of love—none of which bears an expiration date.

Let's now just get down and dirty. How much are you going to expose or give, how vulnerable and open are you going to be or willing to be, how sacrificing and selfless are you going to be if you know that the other person can and will walk out on a whim or be with someone else? The honest and psychologically healthy answer is, "Not much!"

Frankly, women are biologically and psychologically disposed to be nurturers and nesters. Women's bodies are the source of vulnerable new life. When women demean themselves by committing these qualities to a vulnerable situation, they threaten the very core of civilization.

Men are biologically and psychologically predisposed to be protectors and providers. Men's psyches are nourished by having a family to work for. When men demean themselves by committing these qualities to a vulnerable situation, they threaten the very core of civilization.

Oh, I bet you're thinking I'm over-generalizing and getting too dramatic. I don't think so. I've talked to countless thousands of people over the quarter-century I've been on radio—and when the political rhetoric dies down, the truth pipes up: men and women need each other and need to be needed by each other to feel happy and fulfilled. Liberalized modern culture is denying men and women of their most precious goals by telling them that all they really need they can get temporarily and superficially.

Look around you. How many people you know who live that way are truly content and fulfilled?

Don't do what's easy and adolescent; do what's difficult and adult...and deeply fulfilling. Shacking up is for cowards and users. Living together is for married, committed human beings who want the best for each other, their children, and the world.

I'm sorry *Shacking up—40 reasons why NOT to* has to be written—but I'm grateful to Anne James-Sieff for writing this book. My prayer is that her work will help millions regain the dignity and happiness that committed adults have experienced throughout history—and will turn the tide back towards traditional values, without which life loses much of it's meaning.

PREFACE

I was living a pathetically immoral life, skipping along without a thought about whom I was damaging when I left my marriage and started shacking up. My husband, my children, my church friends, and my neighbors were just a few of the people that had been devastated by my imbecilic behavior. My lifestyle choices were made from the depths of narcissism. I was selfish and self-centered. I was hopeless. It wasn't until a few years ago that the full realization of what I had done hit me with a vengeance. The devastation I had rained on so many of my loved ones, for the first time, pierced my soul to its core. I fell into the depths of deep despair and cried almost every day.

I was reaping the ugliness of my choices. I couldn't escape my pain; it followed me even in my dreams. *That is hell.*

I was compelled to write this book. I knew that I *must* write it. If I can help one person change their life for the better, then I have done well.

This book is for all of us baby boomer children, as well as for those of you who are the *children* of baby boomers—and anyone else in-between. It's time we stop and look at what we're doing *and* at how pathetic we've become.

There's an epidemic of "shacking up" going on and it's a disgusting shame. We are damaging ourselves and our society by choosing this lifestyle instead of doing the honorable thing, and that is to commit to marriage.

The reason I wrote this is because I, too, am a baby boomer, and I was shacking up like a lot of you are now—and all I had to say to that was, I made myself sick, and I know that if *I* felt sick about it (and I'm as human as the next person), then deep inside your guts, you feel sick too!

One night while I was driving home I began to contemplate how disgusted I was with myself for lowering my moral standards and "living" with someone I hardly knew! It made me ponder my own self-respect, or rather the lack of it.

When I arrived home, I got the dictionary out and looked up the word self-respect. The definition read as follows: *"Having the proper respect for the dignity of one's character."* I realized that I had none, and a light went on! I went furiously through the *entire* dictionary looking for every word that fit how I felt about my decision to lower my standards. When I was done, for the first time I knew that I was pathetically immoral; I wept, for my children, for my ex-husband, and for myself.

I decided then and there that I had to write a book and address this serious problem with clarity. I thought, how much clearer could I be than to use the definitions of the emotions I have felt as a result of my "shacking up" lifestyle, and then write about it. Thus, *Shacking Up: 40 Reasons Why NOT To!* was born.

We need to get back to the truth of the matter about why we're all choosing this sad lifestyle these days. (In my opinion, we're afraid of true intimacy.) So, the first question I want to ask all of the women who are "cohabiting" out there is this: "What the hell did we do with our morals?" Do we have no shame? How could we just give up our sacredness to any man that comes along, simply because he gives us multiple orgasms or lets us live with him rent free, (and it's really not free at all it's costing you your emotional well being for sure.)…Gag me with a spoon…please!

Oh, and you men! You should have evolved enough by now to think more with your brains and your heart than with your genitals. I think the word I'm looking for right at this point is *maturity*—something many of you men (who are shacking up) are lacking these days, I'm sorry to say! Genitals are much more a priority than doing the right thing…ugh! We've got to get back our morals, NOW. Not tomorrow, not the next day, right this minute before it's too late.

I've written 40 reasons why NOT to shack up, then you be the judge of your own life and the sacredness in which you hold it—because I'm going to tell you, we've all gone wrong somewhere. Many of our kids are using drugs to escape from their (really *your*) reality. They're killing each other and committing suicide. They're bringing guns to school, and girls are getting pregnant at ten, eleven, or twelve years of age. WAKE UP, PEOPLE! They're watching us and we can see the results.

Fathers, your daughters are watching you act totally immoral, starting another life with some other woman that makes you "feel" good. Do you think that little girl of yours is going to find a healthy man (after watching you take advantage of some woman) that will treat her well when she's old enough for a relationship? More than likely, she'll pick a man just like you who will also take advantage of her. Is that what you want for your daughter?

The bottom line is this: we're teaching our sons to disrespect women and we're teaching our daughters to give up their sacredness for a compliment. Is that what we want to teach our children, because when we shack up that's the example they see.

Listen, way too many of us are self-centered, narcissistic babies! If we don't reclaim our sense of morality, our children will be totally lost. Let me ask you something. Do you think what we've been doing is working? *I think not!* We'd better take a long, hard look at where we've gone wrong and start making it right with our children because they are lost and have no respect for us at all! I see it every day, everywhere I turn. Our kids are angry and their spirits are destroyed because of *US*—period!

So, if you didn't like what you just read, then you're not ready to grow up. Your kids will continue to suffer because you're not willing to give up your precious arrangement for the little "nuisances" in your home—and that's exactly how they feel you treat them…like they're an inconvenience!

I'm sick of what I see; I'm sick that I let my own children down. They didn't deserve it. I made a mess out of my life and while I was doing it, I saw so many others doing the same pathetic thing! Finally, one day I woke up…*thank God!* I asked myself, "What the hell am I doing?"

I'm telling you women that if you're choosing to live this way, it's a convenience for him, and he'll always make excuses *not* to get married. Why should he get married? He's getting a freebie: free sex without commitment. Ha…that's so easy, and you, my dear, are such a fool!

I, from now on, will never be willing to lower my standards again. Because frankly, no man is worth serving up my dignity and sacredness on a silver platter so he can have a free-for-all. It's my own fault, and *I have no one to blame but myself.*

I know that if you've been "living" with someone for years, you have risked that precious commodity called time. Maybe you're older now, your youthfulness is fading, and it will be a thing of the past sooner than you want it to be. Then what? You can never get back the time you've lost and finding a mate will only become harder. When your arrangement finally does end, you can bet your bottom dollar that you can be easily replaced. There will be another woman, who's weak like you were, willing to take your place and lower her standards as well as her lace panties (to impress him of her incredible sexuality) because she's sure NO woman can please him like she can—and of course he's not going to argue with a free-for-all! His motto is "NEXT!" and you're left alone—the very thing you feared the most! It's tragic…but a reality!

If you're young and you think time is on your side, and you're just "livin' it up," I'm here to tell you that no amount of money can give you back your dignity once you've spent it on wild living. This may well be a new millennium, but it sure isn't a good one, and you can never get back the time you've wasted.

Think of your life as a bank account: instead of withdrawing and depositing money, you're withdrawing and depositing actions that will deplete or increase your life account. If it's shacking up you choose, that's a big withdrawal, and you have now depleted your moral account (which can never be replaced). Or, let's say you do drugs for ten years; there's another withdrawal from the account of your health. This, also, cannot be replaced—it's gone for good. See my point?

So then, let's say you deposit good living in your life account. The result is a full feeling of peace! No drug can *EVER* give you the peace that comes from good and clean living.

What you deposit and withdraw is of utmost importance. Use every action of your life account for good, clean living. My very dear friend Barbara said something so important to me, and it has made a powerful impact on my life ever since. It sounds simple but if you really think about it, it's profoundly insightful for everyday living. She said, "Anne, I used to tell my kids, 'If you're going to make mistakes, keep them small—they're much easier to fix.'" Is that brilliant or what!! That is so true.

I hope you'll think hard about what you've just read and do the right thing…as much as humanly possible.

So, with that in mind, I will get to it and write my 40 reasons why NOT to shack up! It is my hope that you'll consider this seriously, so we can fix the problem we've created. Maybe we will have time to help our children get back on track. If they see us leave a shack-up situation, then they can see some sort of saneness and hope. The Bible says in Proverbs 29:18, "Where there is no vision the people perish." I would like to rephrase this and say, "Where there is no hope, the children perish." Are we not seeing that right before our very eyes?

We *have* to be strong. They need to see us admit we've screwed up, that we've hurt them, and that we have made immoral choices by having someone just "move in" without the commitment of marriage—lowering our standards for the small pleasure and convenience it gives us.

Come on, everyone; let's turn it all around! As long as we're alive there's hope! We can change this mess we've all made and in so doing, we can turn our precious children into healthy adults who will- have peace of mind, dignity, and morals.

WARNING: There will be no sugar coating of the truth. I'm going to say everything to you that I said to myself when I chose to shack up. If when you read this you become upset or think I'm being too harsh, that's when you know I've hit a nerve, and that nerve is: the truth. That's when you keep reading…

Shacking Up Is

#1 ABHORRENT

ABHORRENT
Causing repugnance, detestable.

A bhorrent means detestable. Repugnance means objectionable and offensive, and that's exactly what shacking up is! I know since you're living with your darling honey you try to ignore that fact, and naturally you're going to pretend that it's okay. But you know in your soul that it's totally detestable.

Let me ask you something; have you thought about those around you and how they're feeling about this? Does it even remotely matter to you? Oh, and by the way, you know that shacking up is still not as acceptable as you might think.

One night, I spoke with a twenty-one-year-old girl who had just been talked into moving in with her twenty-nine-year-old lover, and of course she says that this is a "fairytale relationship." He knows damn good and well what *he's* doing. She's still sweet and green behind the ears. When she talked to me, she practically apologized for shacking up with her lover!

"I know…I always said I wouldn't do it; I'm really a moral person! (Go figure…she's really a moral person!) I never believed in doing it, but I'm so totally in love that I agreed. If there is no proposal in a year from now, I'll move out!"

She's going to move out…get that! After *she* loses her respectability. (I think *he* should feel really crappy about that if the relationship doesn't *happen* to work out.)

"Well, if this one doesn't work, what about the next relationship?" I asked. "Are you going to 'move in' with the next guy?"

"Oh, no! I wouldn't ever do it again!" she retorted.

I didn't get that, "I wouldn't do it again." So, my next question to her was, "Why the hell are you doing it in the first place? Why would you take a risk like that?" How sad I felt for her because she really didn't know the implications of what she was doing to herself.

If you can't see how detestable this is, how objectionable and offensive it is to those around you, then you're in total denial. I *know* that your families are silently objecting on the sidelines, but they don't want to hurt your feelings by telling you so. You know how important not hurting someone's feelings are these days. (It seems sparing someone's feelings outweighs telling them the truth.) I ask anyone out there right now who's shacking up and whose parents know about it (or don't because you're too ashamed to tell them for fear of what they will think), do you honestly believe that this is what they really want for you? Don't you think that they would rather be planning a wedding for their child right about now? Instead, you just can't stand to be without your honey, so you do the abhorrent thing…you move in, not caring about what your family thinks, or what those close to you think about your immoral arrangement, *or* about your own dignity and self-respect!

There was a time when we cared about things like that—what our families thought—especially our grandmas and grandpas. I know I just got a smile out of a lot of you! I could never stand to see how hurt and disappointed my grandma was! Oh God…*not Grandma!*

But hey, just throw out all the caring your family has done for you for all those years, and the life that you lived with them, for your cheap lifestyle. After all, they're not living your life…right? What a sad and selfish society we live in these days. Actually, it is truly…*abhorrent!*

Shacking Up Is

#2 ABUSIVE

ABUSE

To use wrongfully or improperly. To treat in a harmful way.

Abuse. I debated on whether to use the word, but when I reread the definition, it fit perfectly! Shacking up *is* a subtle form of abuse towards yourself and your helpless children, if you have any. Again, let's look at the meaning. Abuse: *"To use wrongfully or improperly. To treat in a harmful way."* Are you going to try and say that this is not the case in your shacking up? After all, doing the right thing would be to marry the person. That's the proper thing to do, but instead you use what should be the intimate institution of marriage for a cheap solution...shacking up! Is that not an improper or wrongful use of what should be sacred? See my point?

Every single person I have *ever* talked to about their shacking up says that they know it's wrong, and they feel bad. So...there's one of the words that describes abuse. Is it proper? Come on now...you know it's improper (After all, isn't that why you picked up this book in the first place, because you know it's wrong and improper...not to mention disgusting?)

Let's look at the last part of the definition...to treat in a harmful way. Okay, be honest now. Don't start rationalizing what you're doing. It *is* harmful to you, and if you have children, it's harmful to them. My hope is that by the time you finish reading this book, you'll really believe that I'm right in what I'm saying. But, I already know *you know* that I'm right and that you're disgusted with what you're doing.

7

One of the reasons why it's harmful to your children is because they learn from you, go out, do the same thing, then get themselves into a disrespectful situation and open themselves up to heartache, pain, and unhappiness—just like you're experiencing right now. I ask you, do you want that for your children? Do you want them to have to deal with all of the pain you are dealing with now?

Your lifestyle is not fair to *anyone!* Please listen to me. I know it's true because I was living proof of it, and it was so painful to know that the man I was living with acted like he had no intention of marrying me.

Do you think that it should have been easy for me to move out after all those years we'd been together? Like I've said before, I was in love all by myself because certainly after all that time, he should have wanted me to be his wife—but he didn't. I was the fool. I'll be the first to admit it! Don't make the same mistakes I made. There are signs all along the way, and if you don't pay attention to them, they will hurt you so much in the long run. Don't just "move in" with anyone *ever.*

As I write this, I cry. Eight long years playing house. How utterly pathetic I had been. I was scared, frozen solid by fear to leave. I kept living with him because the pain of leaving was much harder to deal with than the pain of staying with him. He would always say, "Trust me," but I couldn't. Duh…eight years and no marriage; it was kind of obvious. When I brought up getting married, he treated me like *I* had a problem, when it was really *his* problem. You might ask, "Anne, why did you stay knowing that?" I can tell you it was because I waited too long, and I knew it would hurt so bad. My pride also stopped me. I couldn't stand thinking about what those close to me would think…I could see the word failure in big letters inside my head! Besides, he was charming, and I fell for it.

Now, my eyes are wide open. No man will ever be able to charm me again—I know what it looks like now.

So please, I *implore* you…realize that it is a subtle form of abuse. Turn back from the path you're going down. Make yourself and your kids proud by doing the right thing for them and for all others concerned!

The pride you will have and the sense of well-being will far outweigh any cheap live-in situation you're dealing with. If you had a healthy respect for yourself, you wouldn't be doing it at all. You wouldn't even *think* of lowering your standards for some guy who talks nice but who actually walks very strangely. In other words, he doesn't walk his talk.

If you still struggle to do the right thing—and that is to move out—take out a few pictures of your children, look into their beautiful eyes, and gather strength from that. If you don't have children, go, look at your self in the mirror and say, "I'm worth more than this." Then go get the newspaper and start looking for a new place to move yourself and your children. They deserve the *best,* and you can give that to them. *You* deserve the best, so give it to yourself. *Be strong and do it!* I am behind you 100%. Remember, I've been there and done that! It's painful and so not worth it!

Shacking Up Is

#3 AGONIZING

AGONIZING
To suffer or cause to suffer great anguish.

Well, now that's something I can really relate to. I have suffered incredible pain because I lowered my standards for something fast and shallow. The pain I have lived with from doing the wrong thing in my life ended up not being worth all the fun I was having at the moment. I wouldn't even know where to begin to tell you of the pain I experienced. I can say this though...I have cried many nights and thought about death more than I care to share.

Agonizing, as it says in the definition, means to suffer great anguish. So when you choose to just live together—and you've been in the same relationship for years—you're still not married and you don't know if you ever will be with that person. That's when it starts becoming painful! The suffering comes from not knowing the intentions of your partner.

So, you're in the middle of a fight or disagreement with your lover when out comes that handy little sentence you know they've just been waiting to say. *"That's why we're not married, because we have arguments."* (Adding further frustration to your already uncertain life, I might add.) Or, like when you say, "Could you please pick up the socks that have been laying by your side of the bed for the last three weeks?"

Oops, you shouldn't have said that because you know what (that's right, you guessed it), *"That's why we're not married. I'm not about to get married to my mother; I already have one."* It always amazes me how they don't want you to act like a mother and yet they act like a child, leaving their messes everywhere for their mommy (you) to come and pick up after because they're not adult enough to take care of it themselves! As I always say, "If you don't want a mom, don't act like a child." But that's a subject for another time.

You want to talk about anguish? When you shack up with someone, there's always going to be something you do or don't do that will cause that little sentence to activate. You'll always feel anguish deep inside. Even when you keep busy it will still be there. It's such a gnawing feeling, not to mention painful and irritating. Believe me I know; I lived it. If you've chosen to move in without marriage, you might as well settle into feeling anguish.

I don't know about you, but I have definitely suffered a lot while just living together. I looked up the word "suffer" in the dictionary and it says, "To undergo or feel pain or distress." That fits how it feels to a tee. You feel this vague gnawing in your gut because you know that your chances of really getting married to your lover is a big fat ZERO. If that doesn't cause you deep and troubling anguish, then you're in real denial.

I will name a few things that will cause you to suffer while you choose the pathetic lifestyle you're living. First, you're never sure where that person is emotionally or mentally...NO MATTER WHAT HE SAYS! Secondly, you feel confusion because they say one thing and then do another. For instance, they say things like, "You're the only one for me and I want to grow old with you; you're my soul mate," and yet, when you talk about marriage, they get mad or totally avoid it. So, do yourself a big favor and move out before it's too late in the game. If your "live-in honey" really does love you like they say they do...well, they won't go anywhere and they'll do the right thing, which is to marry you because they do love you. If they don't come around to the commitment phase of the relationship, well, you've been played, honey, straight up. They're in it for only two things: sex and convenience.

Shacking Up Is

#4 ANXIETY-FILLED

ANXIETY
Mental uneasiness caused by fear.

I swear to you that mental uneasiness followed me around like a dark shadow for the entire time I was in my non-committed relationship. It's true when it says that mental uneasiness is caused by fear.

How is fear involved, you may ask? I'll tell you. You will fall deeper in love with him because the minute you have sex, reason deserts you, your emotions take over, and you can't see him for who he really is. When you find out that he hasn't fallen in love with you, that it's just a free-for-all on his end, you're going to experience *fear*...fear of the pain of knowing this is all a joke—and you're the butt of it.

So, you meet someone, you get along really well, and you have a lot in common. You see each other for a few months...Maybe you're older now, you've already been married, and you're just not up for *another* marriage right now, or you just got out of a shack-up situation, (but you don't mind shackin' up again because you just can't stand to be apart).

Usually, he'll make the first move and see if you're *that* kind of woman (easy), so he says, "Hey, why don't you move in and that way you can save some money on rent?" He says it so casually, like he's telling you what his day at the office was like, that you don't notice that this is what he's really asking you: "Hey, I like you, and I want to be able to have sex every night without that heavy commitment...you know, a freebie, so would you like to shack up with me?"

17

It's totally alluring, isn't it? But *you* don't know that you're going to invest *a lot* more than he's ever even going to think about when you move in. For instance, as I said before, you'll fall deeper and deeper in love with him while he keeps his distance so he doesn't hurt too much when you two finally do end it. Remember something very important: *Woman + sex = emotional; Men + sex = physical release.* You're playing with fire, and you're the only one who's going to get burned. Most of the time it *will* end, and you'll have another shack-up relationship down the road. I see it every day with couples. (I did it myself a couple of times, so listen to experience.) They've been in two or three shack-up situations, and I must add that baby boomers are the best at this. Like I said, we started the shacking up trend.

You'll have those mushy feelings, and you'll start thinking of the future with this man. He'll continue to feed you lines of bull to pacify you. (Hey, good term to use for baby boomers!) It's been two or three years now, and you're more serious than ever about spending the rest of your life with him—and you're assuming that he is as well.

I've got news for you, honey, most of the time he's so far from where you are it's pathetic! I know you don't want that kind of pain in your heart. I'm writing this book to help you avoid it. So if he says nonchalantly, "Hey, you want to move in? You'll save money on rent," here's your response: "Rent is a lot easier to come up with than a new heart. Thanks but no thanks." And when you do...I shall take a bow for you. You are awesome!

Shacking Up Is

#5 BLASPHEMOUS

BLASPHEMOUS

Impious attention or action concerning God or sacred things.

When I saw this definition, I debated whether I should use it, but I decided that since it says, an impious action concerning something sacred (like marriage) it *was* appropriate. I know that we hate to be *so* judgmental, and that all things should be equal in value—for instance, that Beethoven and the group "Pig Vomit" are equal in musical talent—but I just don't agree. No matter how you cut it, try to change it, or try to mold it to your belief system, it still comes out the same. Shacking up is an impious action against God, your children, if you have any, your society, but especially against *yourself.* It's blasphemous against the sacred institution of marriage, and there's no other easy way to put it.

It's meaningless, it's empty, and it has no value. It doesn't make any kind of sense, and it ends up hurting the most important people in your life. I'm not saying this to be mean; I'm saying this because I *do* care for you and because I've done it, and I don't want you to go through what I've been through. The pain is just not worth the risk of shacking up with someone who is not committed to you.

When you're sleeping with your sweetie, just remember how impious your action is against *yourself.* This book is for you. It's to tell you that I understand the reasons why you're doing it, and now I'm telling you the reasons why you *shouldn't* do it, based on my own sad choice to shack up for 8 ½ years.

Shacking up=pain. Doing the right thing=peace. Life is too short to live doing the wrong thing or to live in the pain of your poorly thought out choices. Remember this as well: *your choices=your kids' choices.* They have to live with what you choose. I know as a mother I didn't want to choose pain for my children, but they got it anyway because of my immoral lifestyle.

So, change what you're doing to get peace back in your life while you have the chance. It's too late for me, unfortunately, but I'll help you and support you in your decision to have your little friend move out. You just tell him/her that you're going to do the right thing so you can have peace in your life and so that your kids can have peace and contentment too! You are worth the very best, your children are worth the very best, and if someone can't offer you the very best…then you just tell them that they're not the one for you!

Shacking Up Is

#6 CHEAP

CHEAP
Inexpensive, shoddy or inferior.

There was a time when things were wholesome and (I don't care what anyone else says) "Leave it to Beaver" was the best family!

The kids respected the parents because the parents were worthy of their respect. The father was a father, and the mother a mother in *every* sense of the word. Each played their distinctive parts in raising their children. The father was the financial support and firm hand. The mom was a wonderful homemaker and the soft edge to sometimes curb the overzealous dad. There was balance and it felt good—*really* good—and healthy! The boys had their little mischievous side, which is totally normal, and when they got into trouble, they received appropriate punishment and understood why (most of the time!)

Sometimes the parents would make a mistake in the punishment, and they would immediately apologize. They didn't think apologizing was weak or demeaning; it was the right thing to do when they were wrong. Like I said in the beginning, I don't care what anyone says about "Leave it to Beaver," everyone *should* try to pattern their families after them. I don't care if the psychologists analyze that show to death to try to find some hidden ugly dysfunction somewhere in the family—some evil attribute in Ward or perhaps Beaver secretly doing drugs behind his parents' back.

Personally, I think they look for that because that evil is within themselves, and so they try to make everyone else out to be just like them. (I believe the term is called projection!)

"Leave it to Beaver" was a rich, loving, *normal* (in every sense of the word) family—*not* without their problems. Now I ask you, did that family look cheap? Were June and Ward shacking up together? Did the kids pack a gun to school, or did they smoke pot or drink behind their parents' back because they couldn't face the reality that their parents were total shack-up losers? Even though this family was fictional, the message was a good one in that it had high ideals and standards...so what's so wrong with that?

COME ON AMERICA...WAKE UP AND SMELL THE STENCH! We're the ones creating it, and we're the *only* ones who can fix it! Shacking up makes you look cheap and you know it! It makes your kids feel cheap too!

Why would you choose feeling cheap? I also want to add how cheap looking it is to married couples who work hard at their marriages; there's nothing cheap about that! They work hard and deserve all the praise and congratulations for it! They respect themselves enough to give meaning to the process of *true* intimacy (something you're afraid of).

Bottom line...shacking up is cheap and since it's cheap, you'll treat it cheaply—and *you* will be treated cheaply as well.

Shacking Up Is

#7 CONFUSING

CONFUSION
Disorder, lack of clearness, bewilderment.

Bewilderment is a good word to describe how I felt about my "live-in" lifestyle. Bewilderment means to puzzle or confuse *completely*. First, you're told, "I love you; you're the best!" You're also told things like, "I'm so glad that we met," or how about, "I want to grow old with *you*."

That line is sure to make a woman's knees tremble. Here's another good one. "I've never loved any woman like I love you!" That's when you just melt in his arms and you know this is where you want to be for the rest of your life!

Now, if all those lines don't just make your little heart go pitter-patter, I don't know what would. It goes on and on for the entire time you'll be living together. I must tell you though, that there's always a "but" involved in those little sentences. For instance, "I love you, *but* I'm just not ready to get married yet." How about, "I love you, *but* I need more time." I could go on, *but* I won't. He knows that it will take time for *you* to figure it out. When he senses you're starting to, he'll lay it on even thicker so that you'll drop the subject for about another year. That gives him a little more free time. You know, a little more breathing space, a little more free sex without the commitment!

In the meantime, with all the nice little things he says to you (to keep you there, of course), you feel on top of the world! Your step is lighter; you're thinking, *Wow, he loves me more than any other*

29

woman he's been with! That's so awesome. I'm so lucky! *Until*...you mention the "M" word after being together for three or four years. That's when the confusion comes in. "I'm not ready," he says. Your head sort of jerks back and your eyes squint...a swirl of confusion clouds your mind. Did you hear that right? Yup, you sure as hell did! *He's...not...ready!*

But what about all those things he said to you? (It sure seemed like he was ready!) Remember, he wants to grow old with *you* and no one else! You're the best and he's never loved any woman like he loves you! *Yeah, right* is all I have to say to that. The same old lines he's so good at delivering. He's always dishing them out because he knows that that's how he gets his way, and we women fall for it hook, line, and sinker.

Confusing? You're darn right it's confusing, and it always will be with a man who says he's not ready after a certain amount of time. Lack of clarity? Yes, there's a lot of that too! The *only* things that are clear seem to be that you've been strung along, and he's not in it for marriage—period. The lack of clarity comes in when he has said, "I love you, and I want to grow old with you." That makes you think that he *must* be ready to get married. It doesn't take a rocket scientist to figure that out, *right? Wrong!*

Even after he says all those nice, wonderful things, there will always be that little *but* at the end of the sentence and so it forces you to make a move. You start taking things off the walls, while you feel more confused and unclear about what your relationship really is.

You pack your belongings (again) and get prepared to leave, *and* you know that the day you move out, life will be even more unclear than ever. It will be that way for a long time until you heal from the lies and mistrust you experienced in that relationship. You will feel a lot of pain for a while. You're going to *have* to be strong and go through it. You're learning something very important for the next relationship that comes along. You'll be able to see a line of bull a mile away, and will run in the other direction to avoid it!

I'm telling you this because I have fallen for the same lines, and it has caused a lot of disorder in my life. For instance, after being together for eight years it was still not long enough. We *still* couldn't be married; we had to wait *another* year to make sure we'd get along better! It was all so confusing, and I got really tired of it. I was going to have to make a major move in my life because of the utter disorder, lack of clarity, and the bewilderment I kept experiencing in my shacking-up relationship. The countdown had begun; time was running out. No line of bull would work any more. That's when I knew it would be over.

I would have to make my life somewhere else. I was not looking forward to letting go of eight years, but I refused to continue to listen to empty words. I hope you'll think about your situation and all the lines you've been fed to keep you there. You know, honey, in the long run, he's just not worth all that!

Shacking Up Is

#8 CONTEMPTIBLE

CONTEMPTIBLE

A feeling of disdain for anything that is worthless.

Contemptible in Webster's definition has the word disdain in it, so I looked up disdain and it means this: *"To look upon or treat with contempt; scorn; to think unworthy of notice or response."*

That explains why, when I got really anxious about my shack-up honey and I not being married after eight years and confronted him about it, he got irritated. He didn't want me talking about it. That's where I think unworthy of notice or response comes in. "Be quiet about it or just do what you have to do (i.e., move out)."

The subject got talked about a lot in those days because we'd been together for so long it was laughable. When I brought up the fact that I didn't want to live together after that amount of time, that it really tormented me, and that I felt I was just being played with and used, rather than telling me that it wasn't that way, I was met with contempt. He'd raise his voice at me for bringing it up, and I was told that he didn't like being pressured—and so on and so on. Deep inside, I knew he *must* have had disdain for me for not having values enough *not* to shack-up with him, so of course I wasn't treated with the respect I deserved. That's my own fault; I didn't act as if I deserved respect. I moved in with him without being married, and so the value he should have had towards me was lost. Thus, I was treated with disdain.

It's like this: if something of real value is *given* to you (like a brand new Rolls-Royce), do you think you would take care of it in the same you would had you worked your rear end off to get it? You know what the answer is...*of course not!* Well, it's exactly the same thing when you women "just live" with a man instead of being married to him. Sorry, but most of the time he's just not going to treat you the same way because he didn't have to work for it...you get my point?

I dealt with that in some form *every day,* and since I chose to "move in" with him, he naturally had disdain for me deep inside because *I* had disdain for myself. That's the way the psychology works in these matters, as you well know. If I had not disregarded my values and the value I placed on myself, things would have been a lot different, I can assure you. First, I never would have even *considered* moving in with him; second, we would have dated and gotten to know each other; and third, if it had taken him more than two years to ask me to marry him, I would have dropped him like a hot potato.

I had low standards and I got low standards from him as well. So, that's why we weren't ever to talk about how much it hurt me. He didn't want to hear it because then he had to feel crappy about how despicable it was of him to keep putting me off. God forbid we feel crappy about anything we do that's wrong or immoral.

So, if your shack-up buddy gets mad, loud, or even hostile when you bring up the "M" word, this is a sign that, deep down inside, he has contempt for the whole thing. And when you stir it up...it comes out! If you don't mind being treated that way...well then, sadly enough, shacking up is especially for you because you wouldn't do it unless you had contempt for yourself as well. I hate to say this, but you two are a match...have fun!

Shacking Up Is

#9 CRUDE

CRUDE
Lacking culture, refinement, vulgar.

Shacking up is crude. When you do it, you lack culture and refinement. Does it even matter to you that it looks vulgar too? Oh, that's right, we live in a new millennium so anything goes. Hey, why don't we start sleeping with our brothers and sisters while we're at it? How come we don't go there? Isn't the motto, "Do what feels good?" Hey, if someone thinks it feels good to sleep with their brother or sister they should be able to do it!

Why haven't we started doing that? You mean to tell me that sleeping with your sibling is still taboo? Why? That's about the only thing left that is! I'm actually amazed at that! We've accepted everything that isn't normal. We do whatever we want. We don't want any rules imposed on us at all!

I looked up the word vulgar and it says this: *"Characterized by lack of good breeding, indecent, obscene, constituting the ordinary people in a society."* I loved that! So all of you who are shacking up are just ordinary people that are indecent and obscene.

Now please, if we ever meet, look me square in the face and say, "Shacking up is not indecent or obscene!" I'm here to tell you that every woman I know that is doing it feels like they're doing something indecent. Did you read that? EVERY woman I have ever talked to feels that way!

Look, if being ordinary is your cup of tea, hey, it's your life. If being indecent and obscene is something you enjoy, fine; you're only hurting yourself (along with a few important people). But if you want to be *extraordinary* (which means: *"Being beyond what is usual; exceptional or remarkable"*), then living together is something you need to get rid of A.S.A.P. I looked up the definition of indecent and it means the following: *"Offensive to good taste or propriety, unbecoming, unseemly."* You know, I just love looking up words now because it gives me a very clear understanding of the word and how it applies to each situation that we may happen to put ourselves into. How about the word obscene? Let's look that word up. It means the following: *"Offensive to morality or decency. Indecent, lewd, abominable, disgusting."*

So with the definition of each of these words, are you still going to say that your immoral arrangement is not indecent, obscene, lewd, disgusting, and abominable? What is shacking up to you?

Is it beautiful? Wonderful? Heart-warming? A nice thing to do? Does it give you contentment? Do you have peace in your heart while doing it? Are you truly happy? I mean, come on! It's nothing that stands for goodness, values, and morality and you know it. Hell, even gay people who love each other want to be married. If they want to marry because they know it's the right thing to do, then how much more will it take for you to know that it's the right thing to do?

So with that, ask yourself, "Do I like living a crude life for all to see, or do I want to live an extraordinary life?" If you don't want to live an extraordinary life then there's something really wrong with you, and I feel sorry for you. Look at all the definitions I have written in this book. Eliminate each one of them until there's none left. You will feel incredible when you do!

Turn your life into something that you like to look at and that makes you proud! You've got this life as a gift, so turn it into a life that has worth and value for you, your children, and for your family and loved ones.

Start now! Get rid of your low standard of living and replace it with high standards—marriage—and you get rid of crudeness and all the other words that I have written about in this book! That's a lot to accomplish, so go and get busy!

Shacking Up Is

#10 DEMORALIZING

DEMORALIZING

To destroy the morale of. To throw into confusion; bewilder; to corrupt the morals of.

When I read this definition, I hung my head in shame. My heart hurt. What a terrible example I had been to my children and to my children's friends. I destroyed my children's happiness and cheerfulness with my ugly lifestyle.

I went for the moment; I didn't think. I wanted to take a piece of happiness before I died. I didn't realize how I would forfeit peace, security, and contentment (the most important things to have). I did have those things while I was married. What my marriage needed was a good weekend seminar to show us what to do, and we could have made it.

Instead, my poor children watched me while I demoralized my own life. How utterly sickening I was. I can never take back anything now, I can only try to help others choose a different path. My hope is that I can help others to not do the same thing.

So, with that, let me remind you that your children watch your every move. If you're shacking up, your kids will think it's all right. If you're doing it, the first thing they're going to think is that you wouldn't do anything immoral or bad, so then they rationalize by your lifestyle that it *has* to be okay!

Now, would you want *your* child to shack-up with someone? Just picture them coming home and saying, "I'm moving in with so-and-so." Don't tell me that you would be elated…you know you wouldn't be, and if you don't care, then you have some real problems to face about who you are and your lack of morals.

I have been amazed to learn of the way my children watched everything I did, and when they got older, some of things they would tell me about what they remember seeing and hearing shocked me— things I didn't think they knew or saw. I was ignorant; I underestimated their awareness and intelligence. How arrogant of me to dismiss those incredible, trusting souls.

They were watching *everything* I did! They were like sponges, absorbing all the things that were happening around them. We adults taint such innocence without thinking twice about it. We're the ones who cry, "Oh, my childhood was so bad; my parents were the worst," and then we turn right around and do the same things to our own children. It makes me sick to my stomach.

If you're "living" with someone, you are demoralizing not only yourself but your children's future morals and your children's friends future morals as well. If you happen to be a really nice person who almost all of your children's friends like, it's even worse because then they really will be assured that it's okay and acceptable...the normal thing to do.

So, I ask you now, do you want to take responsibility for the children who decide to move in together because they watched you, and you acted like it was okay to do? If so, let that be on your conscience...if you have one. If you do have a small amount of guilt, then run with it to your nearest synagogue or church and start with some counseling from your rabbi, priest or minister. Get your life back on track so your children can be proud of their parents. Please...don't hesitate. As you're reading this right now, walk over to your phone and make that call. Get the help you need to get out of that situation, and when you do, please write me and tell me that you did it! God bless you!

Shacking Up Is

#11 DEPLORABLE

DEPLORABLE
Causing grief and regret, worthy of censure, very bad.

Oy, can I write a book about how deplorable my life has been because of my selfish choice to shack up. I've had so much grief, I couldn't even begin to tell you. It has been extremely hard to live with, but I figure as long as my grief helps you avoid making the same mistakes I have, then my regret and grief will not be in vain.

Regret has been my closest companion these last fifteen years, and I must say it doesn't really ever leave. You can't turn time back and wish it away, and you can't pretend you don't have it; it's always there. You wish that some morning you'd wake up and voila', it's gone! But that will never happen.

I remember a time when I was doing it all right. I had the nice little all-American family; I was a Christian, attending all the potlucks, participating in secret pals, going to Bible studies, the whole nine yards. Life was sweet, I just didn't have the brains to know it.

That's when stupid came knocking at my door, followed by regret, and they've been permanent residents ever since. Taking a long, hot shower won't wash it away. Nothing works. When regret shows up, he always has a pal or two with him, grief being one, sorrow being another, and oh yes, don't let me forget good ol' guilt. We sure can't forget him; he's the leader of the pack.

The four of them have always wreaked havoc inside my heart and head. They go so far as to whisper things like, "Look what you did to your children. They probably hate you for it. You should just end your life so you don't have to live in shame anymore. We don't think you could carry on the rest of your life with this heavy burden of guilt, regret, sorrow, and grief. It's too hard. It's like having a monkey on your back every day. If you take your life, you'll finally get some relief."

I did think of taking my life for the things I have done, but I realized it would be the one thing that would really hurt my kids more than anything I could have ever done wrong in this lifetime. So with that, I became determined to turn my life around and to help others do the same.

Now, let's talk about the last part of the definition of deplorable. Worthy of censure means, *"To suppress anything objectionable."* That's how I lived. I would try to act like nothing was wrong; I would try to suppress my objectionable lifestyle so people wouldn't condemn me. (How stupid was that? As if everyone didn't know.) Mostly, I just ignored what people thought, but believe me, my life was definitely still objectionable to those who were around me while I was acting like an insane fool—especially my family members. It was a tragedy for them, I know.

Moving in together without being committed to marriage does cause grief, regret, sorrow, and it's a really poorly thought out choice to make. It's bad for your mental well-being, and it's bad for your children! It's bad for those that are close to you. So, my advice, based on my own experience, is simply this...*Get out of it—period!* Get some respect back, get some peace of mind, and get some walking orders for him/her. Just do it, and do it right now!

Shacking Up Is

#12 DESENSITIZING

DESENSITIZING

Dull, soften, blunt, deaden, diminish, make insensible, numb, paralyze.

Did you read that? Dull, soften, blunt, deaden, diminish, make insensible, numb, and my personal favorite of all of them...paralyze. Now look around. Doesn't that describe our society to a tee?

That's exactly the effect you're having on the people around you while you shack up. Looking at society today is in no way, shape, or form a pleasant thing. We're all grieving, sadly enough. The more we lower our standards, the more evil creeps in. For instance, the amount of violence in movies. The people who make these movies have gone past the point of no return. What we see these days can make our hearts practically stop right then and there. We went from gasping at, "Frankly, my dear, I don't give a damn!" to disemboweling people! When did we start selling out?

This is for all you Hollywood hot shots who are promoting this garbage. Do you have no sense of shame? Do you not give a damn what you're doing to society? Why do you choose to make movies with so much violence and sex? You Hollywood liberals are the ones screaming about guns this and guns that and we need to ban guns, then turn right around and fill your movies with *guns!* You are the biggest hypocrites with an agenda up the qwazoo!

You're desensitizing our children! You're desensitizing society! The bottom line...you're all money hungry, and you don't care at all

51

about the messages you relay or the children you affect. All you care about is your ego and your bank book. You people are a big part of the problem these days, and it's time you own it! All your money won't fix the damage that has been done by your hands. So live with that!

We've become desensitized to everything. We have chosen to further desensitize our children by our less than honorable lifestyles. If you do it, well, it's really easy for them to do it! Because you choose that lifestyle, you are responsible for dulling, softening, deadening, diminishing, making insensible, numbing, and in the end, paralyzing your children. They will have no sense of shame; they will, in essence, have no conscience and that will set them up for a lifetime of misery!

Like I said in the beginning of this chapter, paralyzing is my personal favorite. Paralyzing is such a powerful word. *I* became paralyzed while in that situation. I didn't have the guts to walk away. I was paralyzed by fear—the fear of breaking up and having him not give a damn because he was just not ready for marriage—but I couldn't spend another eight years hoping.

I was the fool. I saw the signs all along the way and did nothing about it. I was going to have to *unparalyze* myself and walk away before I wasted any more time. It scared me to death. You see, I didn't think about the fact that I would fall in love with what seemed to be Mr. Unavailable. Don't you make the same mistake. The time you waste in your relationship is time forever gone. Remember, he's having a good time, wasting yours. Walk away. You know in your heart that it's the right thing to do.

Shacking Up Is

#13 DESPICABLE

DESPICABLE
Deserving to be despised.

Deserving to be despised. Ahh, now who do you think feels that way right now? You know who I'm talking about. Come on; think hard. Yeah, you know your children despise you for how you're living, and if you don't have children then deep inside, you despise yourself for stooping so low because you don't have the self-confidence to wait for the right person. (The right person meaning the one that wants to do the right thing, and by that I mean marry you.)

But if you do have children, they despise what you're doing. They went from a family to a shack-up situation. Listen, you brought them into this world, and look how you're acting. You're living selfishly. You're a "me first" person! My God, what has happened to all of you?!

Hey, you men out there, it's time for you to grow up! Stop thinking with your genitals and start acting like a man. We need you guys to be strong and protect us from the elements of the world (I don't care if women-libbers get mad right now!). I'm old-fashioned, and I like a man to be a man! I like a man with bigger hands and feet than me. I like that he's stronger than me, and I also happen to like that he has an innate urge to protect me.

You women, you're wimping out. You're getting stupid. You're giving into men, and they're just having the biggest heyday at your expense. Hey, it's on the shoulders of the women to decide whether we allow a man to move in and sleep with us. In fact, the more I thought about this whole scenario, a picture began to formulate in my mind's eye. I see that men have stopped being responsible because we women aren't making them live up to their manhood. Part of manhood is taking on responsibilities, one of which is commitment to marriage. When *we* allow a man to shack up with us, it changes the whole dynamics of the relationship for them, and *we* women are responsible for that. It's time to say, "No, I'm not moving in with you unless we're married." Believe me, things will start changing when we see the part we play in this huge problem.

You men have become like little boys in men's bodies. You have *got* to stop thinking with your hormones and start getting back some respect and dignity by keeping your families together! Doesn't that matter anymore?! Please, I implore you, look at the faces of your children. Don't you see that their hearts are torn and breaking? If you don't have children then look at your parents; can't you see that they are hurt and ashamed by your lifestyle?

Did you *ever* have your heart broken? Don't you remember how much it hurt? Why would you do that to your own children? You men, what are you thinking? Why would you hurt your children so deeply? Just so you could have some hot sex every night with someone you're not even remotely interested in marrying?

You know why? Because you're immature, and you know it. You're still looking for that thrill, sleeping with as many women as you possibly can. The fact of the matter is, you're a man now. You need to do the right thing and that is to stay married.

Your children probably don't even realize they despise you, so I'll say it for them...they despise you. You deserve to be despised by them. H*ell,* you despise yourself! They look to you like you're God, like you can do no wrong. They trust you implicitly; do you know what kind of power that is to have? And what do you do with their love and innocence? You throw it away for some body parts that give you pleasure. *EXCUSE ME*, but what's that about?

This is a call to get it together. Have you ever sat and talked with kids on how they feel about their parents shacking up lifestyle? I have and their hearts are aching with pain. It makes me cry just to write this. They have talked about how their parents let them down when they needed them the most while growing up; how they trusted them and how their parents' minds and emotions were always on their little honey schnoock-ums instead of on them. Their priorities were somewhere else when they should have been noticing their kids crying out in desperation for them!

Something is wrong here, folks! We wonder why our kids are angry, and why they end up going to school and shooting other kids. It is a cry to be noticed, to be heard. I'm not excusing the action, I'm just telling you the symptom behind it. These kids are angry...at us!

Please, I implore you to push aside your desires and urges for some *lasting* satisfaction when you grow older. Knowing that you are a pillar of strength for the children you brought into this world is its own reward, and someday they will be there for you because you taught them the value of doing the right thing instead of giving in to temporary desires and urges. Isn't that the way it should be? Isn't that the ideal way?

Do you really want your children to despise you? Do you really like despising yourself? Look into the future for a moment...You men, you're old now...where are your children? Where are you? You're too old and worn out to chase young women; you're left with just your mind...now what? You women, you've lost your youthful looks, men don't notice you like they used to...what will you do?

I know you know what the answer is because I figured it out myself, and it wasn't to bring shame to my children and to be despised by them for my behavior. How about you? Now go and fix the problem! Don't wait. It's of the utmost urgency! If you care, and I know that you do, do the right thing for everyone involved... yourself included.

Shacking Up Is

#14 DISGRACEFUL

DISGRACEFUL
A person, act or thing that causes reproach or shame.

It's disgraceful to shack up with someone. It causes reproach and shame among your loved ones and friends. (Even though they don't say anything to your face, don't think that they aren't grieving over this decision you've made to lower your self-worth). They *do* feel hurt and ashamed, and if they don't care that you're doing it, then they're just as immoral as you.

Now that I've mentioned your family and loved ones, if you have children, think about how disgraceful it is to drag them along your disgusting path. You think they are indispensable? You think because you gave birth to them, they're just an extension of you; therefore, you can use them at will? They are human beings and although you provided their bodies, God filled it with a unique soul that has nothing to do with you. They came here to complete their mission on Earth; just because you gave birth to them doesn't give you ownership over them!

Why do our children have to get up and see the ugliness of our immoral lifestyle every day? What gives you the right to do that to them? Your job is to guide him or her until they turn 18. You're to teach them right from wrong. You're to feed them, clothe them, and guide them through all the things that life throws their way so they can learn to cope when they turn into adults.

But how in the hell do you think they can cope when you're acting and living like careless, unthinking, selfish adults? Come on, it's time to grow up and start acting like the adult you're supposed to be. Hey, you had your day to have fun, now it's your children's turn. Don't take away your child's only time in life to learn and have some fun. They shouldn't have to deal with your disgusting lifestyle and choices.

Go and do the right thing. Get on the ball. Clean up your act, and after you do that, go up to your children, look them straight in the eyes, and ask them, "Would you forgive me for what I've put you through?" Then promise them that you'll change it and *keep* your promise! If you don't, they'll know you're not to be trusted, and they'll *never* believe you again! Is that what you really want for you and your children?

If you don't have children, is looking disgraceful something that enhances your life? I don't think so! Take the time right here and now to think hard about what you're doing and how it's affecting all of those people who matter to you most. Think about how it's affecting your self-worth. Shacking up is disgraceful and *you know in your heart of hearts this is true.* So...go and make your life right with your children and with yourself—*NOW!*

Shacking Up Is

#15 DISHONORABLE

DISHONORABLE

Loss of honor, respect, or reputation; disgrace. To bring shame or disgrace upon.

When you are honored for something you've done, it gives you a sense of pride, self-esteem, and accomplishment. Knowing you've worked hard to achieve the goal you set gave you great satisfaction in a job well done.

For instance, when you walked up and received your high school diploma, didn't you feel like all that hard work paid off? Not only that, but people came up to you afterward, shook your hand, and said things like, "Wow, I'm really proud of you! You did it; you're awesome!" With that kind of encouragement echoing in your ear, your chest filled with pride from the huge efforts you put out for four long, tedious years! You felt exhilarated, on top of the world!

Then you thought, *I'm going to really show them what I can do,* and you go on to get your Master's Degree or even better, your Ph.D.! Your effort and their encouragement spurred you on to better things! There's nothing shameful about that, is there?

Marriage is another time where congratulations and encouragement are given liberally to a couple. Joy, smiles, sharing, love, and happiness are all too obvious. Do you see any sad faces (except for mom crying tears of joy) at a wedding where two people love each other and *want* to be married? *No,* I don't think so. How about a twentieth anniversary? People come to celebrate all that hard work—it was no picnic for the two involved. It took tremendous determination and plenty of stamina (not to mention tolerance)— some of the attributes you acquire when you commit to marriage and actually stick it out.

Those people that are closest to the couple look at them in amazement and wonder. They are honored by others for all the hard work and sweat it took to make it finally run smoothly. With that in mind, let's talk about your shack-up situation. Do you feel the same sense of pride that a married couple feels for all of their hard work? Don't even say you do because you know it's not even close to the truth!

Now, let me ask you this: did you celebrate the first day you moved in together? Did people come over and tell you things like, "Oh, I'm so proud of you two; you finally decided to shack up together." Did you buy a beautiful cake and have written on it, "Congratulations on our shacking up together?" I don't think so!

You've dishonored the institution of marriage by lowering your standards because it's easier than knowing you have to work through the hard times...and you know it. That's why shacking up is the choice of the day.

It's laughable to me that we have all these books out now about being so spiritual, about doing the right thing so that good things will come to you. No one is reading those books and living by them, that's what I think! It's all too obvious because look at all of you who are living together and not giving a damn about being spiritual and doing the right thing. You strip yourself of honor by taking shortcuts to get temporary satisfaction. I ask you this: *how spiritual is that?*

I know what your problem is; you're weak, self-centered, and your kids are losing the most from your dishonorable lifestyle. You don't even think twice about it because then you would have to face the fact that you've hurt your children and loved ones beyond repair.

So, you want to get back some honor? I know the person you're with doesn't give a damn about *your* honor. Well, here's my advice...you can take it or leave it, but here it is in a nutshell.

Do the right thing: either get married, move out, or have your shack-up honey move their butt out! Give your kids back the honor that they deserve from you—*you owe them that.*

If you're a person without children, then do it for your own honor and for the honor of your family. I love the Asian culture because, to this day, they still live by honor, and it's so refreshing! We would do well to learn from them. So with that, this is what you say...it's a point of a finger and three words away..."Please move out."

Shacking Up Is

#16 DISREGARDING

DISREGARD
Neglect, inattentive, inattention.

Our poor children. They have put up with our crappy behavior for too long! Look at what we're doing! We meet someone after our divorce, we like them, and then it's, "Hey, come on over and move in!" Can I ask you something? Did you happen to ask your children how they might feel about it? I know I didn't ask mine, and I feel so sick about that now! I'm letting you know that your children have the right to have a say in whether or not someone shacks up in *their* house with you!

Think about this for a moment. It's the day your shack-up honey starts moving his or her things in; now picture your children sitting on the couch watching this pathetic charade take place. What do you think is going on in their trusting, little innocent minds? I'll bet you haven't even thought about it, huh. Your children are confused and upset, and you totally disregard them, adding further insult to injury. Their souls are being torn, but hey, I know; you're the adult and you can do what you want, right?

Then, of course, bedtime arrives. That's the moment you and your honey have been waiting for—to hop in the ol' sack and have some unmarried sex with someone you hardly know. Meanwhile, your kids are in the next room wondering who the hell this stranger is you're sleeping with and what the hell happened to their safe home with their mommy and daddy.

Your children are disregarded. You act as if they have no thoughts of their own about it. You don't have the guts to ask them how they feel because they'll tell you the truth; that would burst your little bubble, and you can't have that! You've got to have what you want.

You don't care whether they might not like it or whether it hurts them to see you with someone else other than their father/mother! Disregarded is a good word because that's what you've done to your children. To disregard means to neglect, and that's how they feel right about now. How would *you* like being treated that way? You know how mad you get if your mate ignores or invaldates you and you're an adult! It doesn't feel very good when you really think about it, does it? So please, think about how bad it feels to your child.

Date...don't shack up. You'll sleep better at night. You may be lonely, but better to be lonely with a clear conscience than to shack up and feel guilty with your kids in the next room.

Shacking Up Is

#17 DISRESPECTFUL

DISRESPECTFUL
Lack of respect; rudeness.

This chapter is mainly for us women because *most* men don't care about self-respect when it comes to shacking up. (However, you men can still read this chapter and learn!) After reading the definition above, ask yourself, "Do I have any self-respect, or have I sacrificed it by moving in with a man so I don't have to be lonely and alone after my divorce?" Here's another scenario. You've been with the same guy for say five years, and he *still* hasn't asked you to marry him...but he *has* told you that you could "live" with him. You're older now, so you've just decided, "Screw it. I'll just move in. It's so much easier, and besides, *everyone's* doing it. It's no big deal." I'm telling you, to do so is to sacrifice your self-respect.

Did you ever think that maybe he hasn't asked you to marry him because he knows that he can hold out...but *you* can't? He's the smart one, let me tell you! So, you disregard your self-respect and play house without the commitment of marriage, and you wonder why he won't marry you? Duh!

I know one of the little bonuses of shacking up is that he (maybe) helps you with those annoying little bills you have, which you didn't necessarily have to worry about when you were married.

Do you think getting your bills paid and not dealing with your/his pesky little kids alone (if you two have any) is worth relinquishing your self-respect?

Hey, I realize that being alone is a scary feeling considering we only have a few short years to live on this planet; so we dare not waste any time, even if that means forfeiting our self-respect.

Do you get your self-worth from him because he chooses to live with you, and you feel like, "Wow, he wants ME!"? I've got a news flash for you: he'll take *anyone* who will live with him without marriage. You're no one special to him, believe me! He's really there for the sex, honey, don't kid yourself. Sorry to be the one to break the news to you.

You know what the problem is? Your head is so filled with what you need, what you want, and what you can get that it keeps you from listening to your soul talking. Go into the bathroom right now, look yourself square in the face, and ask out loud, "Do I have any self-respect?" Shh, now be quiet and listen to how you feel. Is there a feeling in your heart that makes you squeamish? A sinking feeling? A slight stab of pain in your heart? Do you see the face of your children flash before you? Do you feel sick to your stomach?

Those feelings are there for a reason; they're there to protect you, and *you're not listening to them*. Instead, you keep busy in the hopes that they'll go away. But they won't, so you'd better change your plans because you're in for more of where that came from, and there isn't *any* deliverance from it except to pack your bags and leave!

I'm telling you this because *I know* what it feels like, and it's probably the most subtle of pains...subtle because we can't look at it head on. We know it's there, so we just keep talking, or working, or drinking, or doing drugs, or just plain filling our minds so full we can't hear it because we just don't want to face the cold, hard truth. We've been duped, toyed with, used, and we're a convenience for someone else.

It's such a gut wrenching feeling. I know, I've had it often enough, and it makes me feel sick just to write this. But I'm doing it in hopes of saving any kind of self-respect *you* have left. Listen, it's not easy at all to make the transition from shacking up because of the convenience it gives you financially.

It's hard to move out after you've gotten comfortable in your less-than-respectable lifestyle, but I implore you to reconsider what you're doing to yourself and your children. There is no self-respect in shacking up, *and you know it!* So please, go…get self-respect back while you still have time.

Shacking Up Is

#18 AN EMOTIONAL ROLLER COASTER RIDE

ROLLER COASTER RIDE

A small railroad that moves along a high, sharply winding trestle with steep inclines.

I was driving past Buffalo Bills Casino at the Nevada state line while it was in the process of being built. On the left side of the huge hotel, a 220-foot roller coaster was being assembled. It looked like a giant toy in the middle of the dessert. Each time we would make a trek up to Las Vegas, I would see it progressing and taking shape. When I saw the final touches being done, I promised myself that I was going on that roller coaster ride, no matter what!

Now, I must tell you that this is way out of character for me...you see, I hate roller coaster rides! They scare me to death! I could not, for the life of me, figure out why I felt so compelled to go on this ride, *until* I started writing this book. That's when I realized that there was a very mystical reason for such compulsion. When I started going through the dictionary and I came across the definition of emotional, the word roller coaster flashed in my head like a neon light across a billboard...I got the chills and really understood in that moment how monumental going on that ride really was!

So, the very next time we made our journey to Vegas, we stopped and registered for a room, as my shack-up honey and I had always done while he did business with a music store up there. As soon as we were done checking in, I went straight to the ride and got in line. As the cars rolled up, there was one with my name written all over it (just kidding). I stepped into the car, and the attendant came over and put the bar down on my lap. My heart started to race like I had downed ten cups of espresso! I couldn't turn back now; I was going for the ride of my life, and I can tell you I was petrified beyond belief.

As it started to ascend, making its way toward the sky with its click-clicking sound, I asked myself in a sarcastically horrified way, "What the hell am I doing; I must be nuts!" It took three to four minutes to get to the top. I could see over the roof of the hotel! I did not want to be there, I can tell you that!

As the cars rolled over the edge and down the drop, it felt as if time had stopped! I was so terrified, I literally could not even scream! I swear I thought I was going to fly out of my seat into the air! We rolled down to the bottom only to be flung back up another 120 feet or so. Then down again, turning so much to the side I thought the cars would fall right off the track. We whipped about fast, wild, up around and down, then back up again, then around. Its speed hit up to 90 miles an hour!

When the ride was finished, and we rolled back into the station, I stepped out of the car. My honey said it looked like I had seen a ghost! When I look back on that ride, I can't help but think, *What a great analogy that would be for the shacking up kind of life.* It's a roller coaster ride—period! It goes up, down and around, then back up again, then down...oy, it makes me dizzy just thinking of it! When you don't know where he/she is at, you can count on this for as long as you live together without marriage.

Not only that, but living with that person is a terrifying ride if you're in mid-life because you're getting older and older, and you have nothing solid built with them.

When it finally does end, it's like that 220-foot drop: you're so horrified, you can't even feel anything at first. You don't want to have to start over again! You don't want to believe it's ending. The pain is like being on that roller coaster ride and having it take you everywhere you *don't* want to go, and *you can't stop it.* You're on it for the ride, but this ride doesn't stop after only 2—3 minutes—it can last for years!

So, you'd better think hard before you get on the roller coaster ride of shacking up because it'll be the scariest ride of your life ...literally!

Shacking Up Is

#19 FUTILE

FUTILE
Having no useful result.

Remember when you first fell in love? What a great feeling! You would sit and talk about your plans for the future for hours on end. It was thrilling for me, I can tell you. We would talk about having children, what we would name them, where we wanted to live, what our house would look like, where we would retire. We loved the mountains—that's where we were going to grow old together. It was exciting, fresh, full of hope, love, warmth, and security. I knew he loved me, and I loved him. I felt strong and safe. He made me feel I could do anything because he loved me.

I have never forgotten how that kind of security felt. I didn't fear the future because my mate and I were going into it together. I wasn't afraid as long as he was there. I have always held that memory close to my heart so I wouldn't forget what it felt like.

My life turned out quite different from my marriage. I could never make long-range plans because I was shacking up with someone who was not (it seemed) on the same page as me after eight years. I was forty-five years old, and every year of those eight years together went by so fast it was unfathomable! I could not plan for my future simply because I didn't know where I was going to be. I didn't *really* know what the outcome would be in my relationship. How can you plan when you're uncertain about the person you're with? It was scary. I felt a lot of futility.

Shacking up dictates to *you* that you can't make plans. Think about it. It controls you! You go day-to-day never knowing what will end up happening. If you're around forty, half of your life is over, and you will live on the edge with nothing to protect you when you're seventy, eighty, eighty-five years old. Think about someone loving you and wanting to be there to protect you when you're in the twilight of your life. There is strength in numbers. Having a mate that loves you is the best thing you could have as you grow old. This paragraph does not include "women-libbers." They're tough; they'll do it alone! I admire them, but most people want a mate when they are growing older! After all, look at Gloria Steinem—she just married. Need I say more?

Please think hard about what you're doing shacking up with someone. Go away for a few days by yourself and really re-evaluate why you're choosing to be unprotected against the future with someone who could care less about you. Time is ever moving swiftly into old age. Where will you be in twenty-five to thirty years? If you get that anxious feeling in the pit of your stomach when you think about it, then you know that you're not in the right place while you're shacking up, and you will pay hard later. Is it worth it?

Take your life back, put security in it, and choose a person who values marriage over shacking up. Choose someone who loves you and wants to protect you. Then you can plan your future with confidence and with someone who has *your* best interests at heart! It's good to know your mate *wants* to be there and wants to make sure you're taken care of when you're old. Shacking up is futile. No useful results can come out of it...*ever*!

Shacking Up Is

#20 HUMILIATING

HUMILIATING
A painful loss of pride or self respect.

Humiliating? I can vouch for that! Shacking up has caused me a very painful loss of pride and self-respect, and I still live with it. It's something that is in everything I do, say, think, and feel, literally every day!

For those of you who don't feel it, well then, you have no conscience and there's probably no hope for you, so don't bother reading the rest of *this* book. Go and do what you want for the rest of your life. But I guarantee you that you *will* pick up this book when your time is finally used up—by that time, it will be too late for you.

Painful as a part of the description of humiliating is such a powerful word for me. I feel pain every day at some level for my past immoral choices and for my recent (past) lifestyle. The day I came to a full realization of what I had done, and how it had affected my children, hit me so hard I thought my heart would literally burst. I called my ex-husband first and while I cried uncontrollably, I asked him if he would forgive me for the pain I'd caused him and for the things I'd put him through. Then I talked to each of my three children and asked them to forgive me as well. Even though they did, it still didn't take away the ugliness of the humiliating past I had lived. I can never remove the scars that have settled in the hearts of my children. They will be there permanently, for the rest of *their* lives. What did they ever do to deserve to have to live with the things *I* have done?

But they will, and that saddens me. However sad, this one thing remains true, what's done is done. There's no turning back.

I never thought that what I did could have that much impact on my children! I can't believe that I didn't think about it! I was crazy! I went out of my right mind! I went from moral to immoral in the snap of a finger; I wasted no time. In my heart now, I long for things to be the way they used to be when I was married. I don't want to feel this humiliation anymore. The only relief I will get from my painful loss of pride and self-respect is when I die, plain and simple.

Don't let that happen to you. Once you let your morals down and you shack up, you will feel the humiliation of it, not to mention the humiliation your kids will feel. It's a no-win situation, and changing it will be very difficult once you've set your actions into motion.

If you don't have any children, you need to look around and see who is watching you shack up. You *are* affecting someone and they might make the decision to shack up because they admire you and think that if you do it, it's "cool." Please look around; see who is watching. Do you want to be responsible for someone else making an immoral decision to shack up because you're doing it?

Think hard about what you're doing. If you're considering shacking up, I'm glad you've picked up this book because I'm here to tell you...*DON'T DO IT!* Save yourself the humiliation. If someone asks you to shack up, they don't have your best interest at heart! *Know that!*

Shacking Up Is

#21 ILLUSIONARY

ILLUSION
Something that deceives by producing a false impression of reality.

If you're a naive kind of woman and you've been subtly talked into shacking up (by the way, here's the definition for subtle: *"Difficult to perceive...cunning or crafty"*), wow, are you in deep trouble! He's got lines for you that you couldn't even dream of. Remember, he has to use them to get what he wants without you suspecting an ulterior motive...and you know what the motive is, of course—SEX...without the commitment.

I'm writing this to let you know that it's all an illusion, babe, and he's the biggest part of it! Read the definition again...something that deceives by producing a false impression of reality. There we go! Men, I hate to say this, but you guys do a lot of double-talking and deceiving to get your way *and* you even believe your own lines. It took me a long time to figure it out and *not* without the heartache it takes to do so. (I had to get rid of my naivety first and not be so trusting about what I was being told.) Now let me clarify: there are men who don't deceive and I commend you for that—obviously this chapter is not for you. This chapter is for the men who deceive women every step of the way, and you all know who you are. *SHAME ON YOU!*

Now, in the definition it says that illusion means you produce a false impression of reality (to get what you want, of course). You have a little fun for a while because it's a freebie with no commitment. You don't have to worry about being called a slut or loose. So, all the way around you're havin' a grand ol' time at the expense of someone else!

Right at this juncture I need to include the women that use men for financial gain—women who live with a man and give him hope that the two of you might go somewhere in the future when you know, in fact, you're not planning a future at all. I know there are women out there that do this, and it's really a shame when the man wants to be married and you lead him on knowing you have no intention of ever fully committing to him.

As I said, it's all an illusion and it's so sad for all involved. It's game playing at its finest. It's living a lie. It's deception. Do you want to live a lie for the rest of your life? Do you want others to deceive you as well? How do you expect anyone to believe you if you're always lying and deceiving to get what you want? When you finally decide to fix it, people will no longer believe anything you say.

Eventually, you will fall in love with someone and maybe then you'll be lied to by her/him; you'll be given hope, just like you gave someone hope, but it will all be a lie. Remember, cause and effect are always at play, and they will balance the scales of your actions. You will not be able to run from the very things you used to do to others. The universe is giving back what you gave; that's how God designed it. So, think hard about what you're doing. Make the right decision. Don't shack up with someone; it's selfishness and narcissism at its finest. Marriage takes two mature people who believe in truth, honesty, and sacrifice for the good of the whole.

Shacking up is an illusion. Remember, it means "something that deceives." That's what both of you are doing to each other...what a shame. I grieve for you that you don't have what it takes to love deeply, or to risk the fear of intimacy for what it will end up offering in the end...depth and having someone know you so well that when you look at them they know exactly what you're thinking. When you hurt, your mate hurts as if it were happening to them. Your souls blend. It's when you can't tell where you begin and they end.

Just living together can *never* offer you true intimacy, and you know it. Seek the truth in the relationship, the truth that it's a lie you're living. I have always said, "I seek truth over comfort." Shacking up can be comfortable, but it's not the truth. It's the ultimate illusion *against yourself.*

Shacking Up Is

#22 INSECURE

INSECURE

Subject to fears and doubts. Exposed or liable to risk or danger. Not firmly or reliably placed or fastened.

Fear and doubt are the feelings I learned to live with *every day* of the eight years I shacked up. My fears had built to such a pitch that if he whitened his teeth and had a place to go in a hurry, I would be tormented for hours upon hours, if not days, with what I thought he might have been doing.

All my sensibility went out the window and my imagination ran wild! *I hated it!* The danger, I felt, was that I was not firmly placed in a secured, committed marriage where I knew my mate wanted me and proved it by taking the vows of marriage.

Instead, he avoided it. It made me wonder that if *I* wanted to be married to him, then why didn't *he* want the same? And that's where the feeling that I wasn't secure came in. I saw that he didn't want the deepest kind of intimacy that marriage could offer, so then I was again forced to ask myself another question: "What am I doing with him if we aren't on the same page?"

He wanted an arrangement; I wanted intimacy. Shacking up is not deep and intimate because of the lack of commitment. It's a test run. You always have an uneasy feeling in the back of your mind that the relationship is not stable and that one day, your lover will come home and say, "Well, I'm in love with someone I met online, and I'm moving out."

I know someone personally that did this to the woman he had been shacking up with for twelve years. He started talking online with some other woman; they decided they wanted to meet and did. He went to the Midwest for a week, came back, and told his honey he was leaving her.

His long-time lover had come down with MS (multiple sclerosis) years earlier, and she was disabled. It had advanced to the point where she was falling down. He didn't care; he packed up, left, and married this other woman a week after he got back to where she lived! Obviously, being married was important to him after all.

He said this to me about his shack-up lover: "She's just a body to keep me warm and a place to go on the weekends for a good meal." A tragic story when you settle for less than the best. At least in marriage you're both saying, "Okay, I love you very much; you are the only one for me," and you seal it with vows to each other. There is security in that or people wouldn't get married at all.

Shacking up is not reliable. I want you to look at the differences between choosing that lifestyle versus marriage. When a person loves someone, they don't want anyone else; they want them to always be there "until death do you part." Then those two people take a vow to prove their intent to each other. If they marry when they're older and wiser, their chances of understanding how to make the marriage work are increased, and the chances of a stable, long-lasting marriage are *secured!*

The definition of insecure states the following: *"Not firmly or reliably placed or fastened."* That's what shacking up brings to the relationship. Unreliability…does that sound like something you want to live with every day? Not knowing if your honey will want you in the end? Shacking up is risky business; lots of people get hurt, but mostly the children get the short end of the stick.

Obviously, there are differences between shacking up and marriage. Marriage offers security between two truly committed people. Shacking up offers insecurity, fear, doubt, risk, and the possibility of danger (i.e., AIDS or other sexually transmitted diseases), and it is nowhere near reliable. Shacking up is always an open-ended deal.

Now you choose. What do you want? Marriage, where you are truly wanted by the person, and they are committed to you and are anxious to take vows of love, security, and faithfulness? Or do you choose the road widely traveled by many these days...shacking up where no vows of love are taken, you are at risk with all the things I named above, and in the end you have a broken heart.

We all know what it is to wake up after you've broken up with someone you've been with for a long period of time—it's a killer! You can't think, you can't eat, you wake up every hour on the hour crying your eyes out! I know—I went through it!

So with that, I hope you choose the best for yourself, which is marriage to someone who doesn't love himself/ herself more than you, and someone who has the highest standard for you and your children (if you have them). Don't settle for anything less, or that's what you'll get...*less* than the best.

Shacking Up Is

#23 MEANINGLESS

MEANINGLESS
To have no purpose, significance or importance.

Can you tell me what meaning there is in shacking up? Please, just sit and really think about this for a while. What significance is there in it? Does shacking up bring importance to your life and the lives of your children? What purpose does moving in with a bunch of different people offer you?

The reason I say a "bunch of different people" is because chances are, you're not going to have just one shack-up situation. In fact, most likely you are in your second one now, right? Once you do it and it doesn't work out with that person, it's easier the second time around; we all know that's true. It's like that with anything…doing drugs, sleeping around, etc. So, have you thought about my questions in the opening paragraph? What meaning is there in shacking up with someone?

What significance is there in it? Does it bring importance to your life and to the lives of your children? What purpose is there in it? What does it offer you? Does it enhance your life? I *know* that no person in their right mind would want a life without purpose, significance, or importance…right? So now is the time to ask yourself, "What am I doing in this lifestyle?" You certainly don't want a life devoid of meaning, so you have to decide right here and now that you're going to get back true meaning and worth in your life by doing the right thing. Self-esteem doesn't come from loving yourself so much as it comes from accomplishment and doing the right things in life.

Accomplishing things that have meaning and worth are not always easy; in fact, the best things in life are hard to get. That's just the way it is. Think about this: Let's say you're a lawyer now. What did it take to get there? I know right about now you're saying, "If only you knew!" Believe me I do; I worked for enough of them. It took a lot of hours of studying and staying up till dawn for years to get to the end result. Then there was the bar exam, which you still had to pass *before* you became licensed.

We can use example after example of people who had to work hard to get to where they are because anything with *VALUE* takes lots and lots of hard work. Anything with meaning does too! Marriage takes a lot of hard work by two people who know what true commitment is. Let's just put it this way: *marriage=depth and meaningfulness; shacking up=shallowness and lack of meaning.*

Let's start to really rethink what we're doing, baby boomers, and anyone else that has lowered their standards by shacking up. We need to pull ourselves up by our boot straps, clean up, and get some real meaning, purpose, significance, and importance back into our lives! We're going to have a good night's sleep when we *know* every day that our lives are clean, our conscience is clear and everything is in order as it should be.

Start now and be the example for others. Get your life back on track. And while you're at it, put a sign on your front door that reads: NO SHACKING UP ALLOWED HERE! That will be for your date to read. He'll get the message that you're a person with high values, and he'll respect you for your stand!

Shacking Up Is

#24 PREPOSTEROUS

PREPOSTEROUS
Completely senseless or foolish.

The word preposterous dumbfounded me when I read the definition! Completely senseless and foolish! I could end this right here and now, but I'm not done with you that quickly—or with myself for that matter. I need to make you feel so crappy about shacking up that by the time you read this chapter alone, it will make you hightail it right out of your senseless and foolish lifestyle!

Can you really say that doing it *isn't* senseless or foolish? Say it out loud right now…"Shacking up is not senseless." Say, "Shacking up is not foolish!" Oh man, you are delusional if you really believe that, but I know you really don't! (If you're honest with yourself.) Okay, let's say you *do* believe it. Name a reason why it makes sense or isn't foolish. Can you, without having a feeling of shame in your heart?

I looked up the word senseless; here's what it says: *"Unconscious."* (That one made me laugh, because that's what we become when we shack up!) Then it goes on to say: *"Stupid, meaningless."* Need I say more about what that kind of life offers two unconscious people?

Hey, if you don't mind knowing you're stupid or unconscious, or that you're foolish, (according to the dictionary) I say, have the time of your life because you don't know the difference anyway! You've just resorted to being an animal instead of a human being! If what I just said made you mad…then I've done a good job. You've got to rethink what it's doing to society in general, but most importantly what you're doing to yourself.

You know what elevates you from an animal? It's the fact that you know what is right and what is wrong. You know the difference between good and evil. You know when you're clothed and when you're naked. You know how bad it feels when someone hurts you, and you also know that you can hurt others in return. But we have turned into animals doing whatever we want, not giving a second thought to whom we're hurting, how ugly shacking up really is, and the damage it has done and is doing to ourselves and everyone watching.

In my religion, Judaism, it teaches that man did not fall from grace as the Christian religion teaches, but that it was the ascent of man to awareness. When "Eve" took the fruit of the "Tree of knowledge of good and evil," her eyes were opened, and she became aware that she was now different from the animals, separated from them. That moment made her an intelligible human. At that moment, she also knew she was naked and needed coverings.

We, as humans, can tell that there is something different about who we are compared to the animals. We find a mate, we fall in love, and we automatically want to be married. That's just the natural order of things...that's just who we are. Shacking up is like being an animal; you have sex and hang around for a while until it becomes too difficult or boring in the relationship, and then, like an animal, you leave for the next sex partner.

Don't get me wrong, I know that we're part of the earth (part animal), but we're also part of God (having his ability to be aware and know the difference between good and evil). It's time to elevate ourselves, and the way we do that is to do the right thing—be different from the animals.

Remember, the definition means to be completely senseless or foolish...completely. There's no if's, and's, or but's about it... shacking up is preposterous!

Shacking Up Is

#25 SACRILEGIOUS

SACRILEGIOUS
Grossly irreverent toward what is sacred.

Reverence means to have deep respect tinged with awe. Shacking up with someone doesn't even come close to being reverent, and it's certainly not even in the league of awe.

You think you have reverence for the person you're living with? Really? *I don't think so.* You couldn't possibly be feeling awe towards the person you're playing house with!

Bottom line? Two people who truly love each other want each other equally. They can't be without the other for too long and each wants marriage as much as the other. They're the ones who have a sense of reverence for each other, and they also hold each other in awe—that's why marriage is so important to them.

Each is saying to the other, I want you, I need you, no one else matters—and so they're not afraid of marriage! Marriage is nothing to be afraid of *if* you can trust *yourself!* If you can't, then you need to step aside, rethink what you're doing, and fix it.

So, take a long look at what you're doing and as always, let me remind you again that your children will also learn irreverence from you if they see you just living with someone. They automatically *know* that it's irreverent without being told! Ah…that's the beauty of children; they see things the way they should be seen…in all its truth!

Now, go and move out of your cheap live-in lifestyle, and change your life to one that has reverence—reverence for other people and reverence for *yourself.* The only way you can do that is to marry the person you are with, and if you don't love the person enough to get married to them, don't keep them there believing a lie. Tell them honestly you have to move out because you don't have any intention of marrying them. At least give them the dignity they deserve.

The last thing I want to say is, if you believe, like a lot of baby boomers do, that the universe gives you back what you have given…well, you're in a whole lot of trouble because you won't be getting a whole lot of reverence back anytime soon for what you've been doing. What you give is what you'll get back. Plain and simple…cause and effect *are working on you!*

Shacking Up Is

#26 SAD

SAD

Sorrowful; unhappy. Causing sorrow or gloom.

I cannot help but think about those around you that are being affected by your lifestyle. (As I say, your children most of all.) If you don't have children, then how about your mom and dad? How about your grandma and grandpa? How about your brothers and sisters? How about your friends, who knew you and your husband or wife? I'm sure they know what you're doing, even if you're not living in the same neighborhood now. Word gets around; you can count on that!

I can tell you from my own personal experience what I went through. It's difficult to think about it now, to see me go from a respected mother, wife, and devout Christian, to a total shack-up loser. What a nut case I was!

The neighbors across the street and to the side of me thought I had lost my mind (which of course, I had). One day, when I was getting into my car, the neighbor woman, whom I had known for years and who knew my children when they were toddlers, was standing on her porch. When she saw me, she made a really crude comment about how I was living at the time. Of course, I had to defend my position and, most importantly, save face. (The only problem was, I hadn't realized I had no face left!) I went up to her and told her that if she weren't so old, I would have kicked her rear end. (Well, my language was actually much more like a drunken sailor on a late night drinking binge!)

That's how far I had stooped to justify what I was doing. I can't tell you how incredibly stupid I feel now, looking back on how I acted that day towards someone who had cared deeply for me and my family so much. I have since gone to them and apologized for my insane behavior.

I know that they were grieved and sad because I broke up my marriage. They could see that my poor children were suffering. But no one could have changed my mind. I was hell-bent on getting what I wanted; I didn't care whom I hurt or made sad while doing it. Hey, no one paid a damn bit of attention to me, so I figured no one would notice what I was doing. I was so wrong to assume that! It's amazing...when you're doing the right thing, no one says a word! But as soon as you do the wrong thing, *everyone* notices and has something to say about it!

Now, when I see people tear their families apart, I feel grief and immense sadness, just like the lady across the street. *Now* I understand. God, I want to scream at everyone who is tearing their families apart because of sheer selfishness! I want to shake them and yell, "Grow up, dammit! Just stay married and work it out for God's sake!"

The people that you are hurting and causing sadness to by shacking up won't tell you so; they don't want to interfere or make you mad. But go up to someone you've known for a long time and ask them to tell you honestly if what you're doing saddens them and see if they don't answer you with, "Well, yeah, I do feel sad (but quickly add), but I just want you to be happy." The last part is so you won't feel guilty for what you're doing. They don't want you to get mad at them, and they don't want to feel responsible for you feeling guilty that you're shacking up.

If you care even remotely for your children and for your loved ones, have the guts to call a meeting and have an honest talk with them and see what they *feel*. You'll be surprised if you let them be honest with you. Maybe it would help you see how despicably you're living, and it will cause you to change it. Of course, the change will be for the ultimate good of all and *everyone will win!*

Shacking Up Is

#27 SELFISH

SELFISH

Caring chiefly for oneself or one's own interests...regardless of others.

Selfish, that's what you are. You're only thinking of yourself and no one else. It's selfish no matter how much you try to cut it, slice it, dice it, or whatever else you want to do with it, so you don't appear to be totally self-absorbed. The definition says you care chiefly for yourself regardless of others and how they might feel.

If you have children, how do they feel about what you're doing with some woman/man that has replaced their mother/father? Oh, that's right, you hadn't noticed because you're chiefly interested in yourself. You could care less about their feelings. You're selfish, unthinking, and uncaring about anyone you affect.

If you took all that energy in being self-absorbed, all that energy in chiefly caring for only yourself and your self-interests, things could really turn around for the good. Here's a scenario: let's pretend that every single person that's shacking up, stops doing it. Wow, what a huge statement that would make to our broken and hurting children, wouldn't you agree?

If you're shacking up for financial reasons and you're a woman, you can take care of yourself just as well with a female roommate, and you know it. You'd even have some dignity to spare because you'd have peace of mind knowing you're not degrading yourself for some man who's foaming at the mouth to get a piece of you every night.

119

If you're a man...sex isn't everything! Learn some self-control; put all that sexual energy into something creative that will have a positive outcome...like martial arts. There you will learn about being more spiritual, and you will also learn to control your impulses! It's sad that we just don't care about anyone but ourselves. I'm going to say this until *you* get blue in the face from hearing it so much: "Shacking up is selfish!" If you love your children, even a little, STOP DOING IT!! Nothing good comes from shacking up...*nothing* at all. Let's get a grip on ourselves.

Let's put aside our selfishness and start doing the right thing, the moral thing. Let's give our children back some peace of mind. What have they ever done to you that they should have this lifestyle forced upon *them?* So, now that you know you're selfish, what are you going to do about it? I'll tell you what you're going to do, fix it today! Right now, get on the phone and start making arrangements to move out. Call a good friend who will support your decision and help you out of what you're doing. When your honey bunches comes home tonight, sit him/her down and give them the bad news!

It will either be, "I'm moving out this weekend," or "You're moving out this weekend." Either way, someone is movin'... PERIOD!

Shacking Up Is

#28 SHAMEFUL

SHAMEFUL
The painful feeling of having done something dishonorable or improper.

Shame, isn't it such a great feeling to have? Yup, now that's the feeling that motivates me in the morning; how about you? Hey, what's even better is to have our kids wake up in the morning and see us coming out of our bedrooms where we slept with our shack-up honey the night before, and then try to act all sacred about it...*that is so laughable!*

There's nothing like good old shame. Look at the top of the page again and see what Webster writes about shame: *"The painful feeling..."* It also states: *"A cause for regret or disappointment, to suffer disgrace."* Well, I can tell you that the only people feeling pain, disappointment, disgrace, regret, and dishonor are your children, along with your loved ones and friends. You're too damn wrapped up in yourself to feel it! It would ruin your convenient little arrangement with your "live-in," and you can't have that!

You men have it made in the shade and you women just "give it up" to keep that man in the house. We've made a pact with the devil; we serve our children up on the altar of our egos and desires so we can grab little tidbits of false happiness and companionship, and of course we can't forget that all important word—that one word that brought us together in the first place—*SEX!*

There's no use in denying it either, because you all know it's the reason you got together and since we're on that subject...you're not with each other because you really truly love each other (or you would desire marriage over living together). You are not together because you're truly committed to each other (or you would have gotten married). You are not together because you're best friends, and you just can't stand to be without each other (if so, you would have walked down the aisle and taken vows of marriage).

You know damn good and well in about three to five years you're going to go your separate ways. There'll be no marriage and your children will disrespect you even more in the end!

So, go ahead and have your temporary fun at your children's expense, and if you don't have children, at your parents' or your siblings'or your beloved grandparents' expense. They were the generation who actually coined the phrase "shacking up," and it makes them sick to watch these charades go on, I'm sure.

You watch and see what happens down the road; it won't be a pretty sight. Oh, and by the way, when it doesn't work out and they go and find someone else, don't forget to start your new "live-in" arrangement with another lover (because that's what almost everyone who has shacked up before usually does). After all is said and done, don't you dare expect for your kids to listen to or believe *anything* you have to say; they just flat out don't care about your opinion, and why should they? It's not based on anything of value.

The very act of shacking up invalidates what you have to say, and don't give me this, "Well, I'm the parent and they're my kids." Yeah, well if that's the case, then start acting like you're a parent. Start by acquiring some morals. Move out of your dishonorable arrangement, and reclaim your children and your parental rights. Until then, you have no right to preach to your children—so just keep quiet!

Shacking Up Is

#29 SUSPECT

SUSPECT

To distrust or doubt. Open to or viewed with suspicion.

The word suspicion comes from the root word suspect. When you choose to just "live together," it starts out as a very casual arrangement...until one person gets more deeply involved (usually the woman). That's when trouble starts brewing and suspicion is part of that trouble. I'll use myself as an example.

My shack-up fiancée said I'm the only one that he wanted to be married to...but it never happened, even *after* eight years. Go figure! So, what do you think I was thinking when he would say, "Oh, I have to go to Las Vegas," and it happened to fall on a day that I couldn't go. Seems convenient, huh? And this would happen quite often.

Or how about this one: he goes to get his hair done every so often by a woman he dated once or twice, and has known for 15 years, and she's still single. (Well, shacking up right at the moment—but still single for all intents and purposes.) He shaves and cleans up real nice, and sometimes he even puts on *my* favorite cologne. How am I supposed to react to that? After all, he still hasn't married me; what's there to trust in that?

He would always say, "I want only you," but, again, after eight years we still hadn't gotten married. I felt so confused...hello! He always reassured me that, "You can trust me," but that didn't stop the war that raged in me when those things came up.

I always had a small or sometimes large (usually after a fight) amount of suspicion; it's something I couldn't help. I always felt uneasy deep inside because I was being put off. I knew it, and frankly, I loathed it!

So be prepared if you're thinking about shacking up or you just moved in with someone; you're in for a whole mess of problems that you're really going to end up regretting. Shacking up offers no guarantees, and the guy you're doing it with knows this a lot better than you. He keeps his emotions out of it, that's why! For women, on the other hand, keeping our emotions out of it is like trying not to breathe—we just can't. Unfortunately, that's the way we're built; it's something we can't help. It's kind of like how men are visual. Telling men not to be visual is like telling us not to be emotional.

So, if you still think it's a wise move on your part to shack up with some guy, go ahead and make that really dumb move—but don't say I didn't warn you! You're going to gamble and lose. These are just the cold, hard facts.

Shacking Up Is

#30 TRAGIC

TRAGEDY

An unfortunate or dreadful event or affair, a drama dealing with a
serious or somber theme, ending in disaster.

When I picked up the dictionary, I looked at every single word in
it. When I came upon a word that hit me in my heart, I knew it
applied to me, and that would be the word I knew belonged in my
book.

Tragedy fit perfectly. It is how I have felt about my own
despicable, immoral, ugly, sad lifestyle. Tragedy is one of the words
that I picked out and the reason I did so is because I have seen what
shacking up has done to us, thus, the word tragedy is as descriptive as
it is precise. You see, it is an *"unfortunate, dreadful* (for the children
and other important people in your life) *event or affair. A drama
dealing with a serious or somber theme."* What could be more serious
and somber than watching your children just about die inside when
their homes fall apart, and their beloved parents, who once loved each
other, part ways?

Shacking up is almost always the next step after a separation and
divorce! It says at the end of the definition that its ending is
disastrous. I have to admit, it is almost always a disaster. Most of
you who are doing it have done it a couple of times, as I've mentioned
before. How many times are you going to shack up with someone
before you realize that it is going to end in pain and sorrow?

The children are not usually allowed to tell you how much pain
they're in. Do this for me if you're thinking about shacking up. I

131

challenge you to go into your child's room and just flat out say, "I want to move in with Joe blow; do you think it's right or wrong for me to do this?" Say to your child, "You can be honest. Tell me how you feel about me doing it?"

I guarantee you that your child will say, "No, it's not right." Now, how do you think that they know that it's wrong? They haven't lived long enough or even know what an adult knows, yet they know instinctively that it's wrong to do.

So, I challenge you to talk to your children before taking that scary step of moving in together without being married. Unfortunate and dreadful events are lurking right around the shacking-up corner, and its ending will be a disaster. You know it's true in your heart, so stick to the straight and narrow. Yes, it's less exciting, but much safer for you and all your loved ones!

Shacking Up Is

#31 UNCERTAIN

UNCERTAIN

Not precisely known or fixed, not confident, unstable, not reliable or dependable.

Uncertainty...shacking up...uncertainty...shacking up. Hmm, now those two words just fit together like a nice little puzzle.

Uncertainty means that something is not precisely known or fixed; that's a great way to describe shacking up! Here's another part of the definition: *"not confident."* Now, you know I'm talking about you and your despicable lifestyle. Unstable, unreliable, and undependable! Those definitions fit what shacking up will offer you.

Instability is a good word for the kind of life you will live. When I told my shackup honey bunches that I would be moving out if we didn't get married, my comment was met with silence...that was not a good sign. You don't think that felt unstable to me? You don't think that felt unreliable and undependable? Most of all, we were not on the same page.

You don't think it scared me so bad that I got mood swings that were unexplainable (at least to him)? The simple truth is, *they weren't for no reason;* they were happening because of the fear and dread I had that after eight years there would be no marriage. I wanted badly to push it so far down inside me that I wouldn't see it for what it truly was—*convenient for him.*

There is no worse feeling than knowing that the person you're just living with is undependable. When you choose shacking up, it's like you're being test-driven, and if they don't like the way it feels well...*next.* You're out of luck, *and* your children watched with their beautiful, innocent eyes while you lost your morals. I grieve for those children. I got that sinking feeling like I knew he wasn't going to stop me from moving out, and I wasn't sure he was going to marry me either! So then what do I do? You can't rely on whether your life with this person will be permanent one day or off the next. I know what you're thinking right now. "Well, marriages can be that way too!" Okay, you're right. Nowadays, that *is* true, *but it shouldn't be.* It wasn't that long ago in the past when people stuck it out and just worked at it. That "piece of paper" meant something. It wasn't just a piece of paper, it was a contract, a sacred vow taken in front of God, your family, and your friends that you would stick it out.

The strength of society depends on the strength of the family. Our *ideals* will make or break us as a civilization. I looked up the word ideal and here is the definition: *"A conception of something in its perfection. An ultimate aim. Regarded as perfect."* In the book, *Jews, God, and History,* by Max Dimont, it states that three highly regarded philosophers make an observation that civilization is not a series of isolated happenings but a flow of events having continuity. Each civilization follows a more or less predictable pattern. They think each civilization is a living being, which, like a human being, has an infancy, adolescence, maturity, old age, and death. How long a civilization lasts depends upon the ideas and *IDEALS* by which that civilization lives. They say that civilizations go through the spring of early origins, mature into the summer of their greatest physical achievement, grow into the autumn of great intellectual heights, decline into the winter of their civilization, and finally die.

The book goes on to further state that western civilization is in the winter of its cycle and will die by the twenty-third century. It doesn't take a rocket scientist to understand just how far we are into that decline. (I shudder just to think about it.) We will be superseded (or taken over, invaded, whichever word you feel more comfortable with). We are seeing the erosion right in front of us. We have lost our ideals and our morals; we've replaced them with convenience. How many of you out there have high ideals for yourselves? How many of you expect only the very best performance from *yourselves* towards your mate? There was a time, that very first time you knew that person was the only one for you, when you would later utter those famous words, "Until death do us part."

True intimacy is the place in which your soul will grow the best. If you're spiritual, this statement will ring true for you. If you're not so spiritual, then marriage will turn you into a better person if being a better person is what you're striving for. Building intimacy takes time and a lot of trusting and hard work. Intimacy was what people built back when we believed in staying together. Now we just toss out the whole thing. Our laws have made divorce easy. Thus, we have people married three, four, five times and think nothing of it now.

Marriages are permanent, if you choose for them to be. It's all up to you and your mate to make it so, it's only a thought away. It takes strength. Are you strong? Because I'm not seeing strength of character in very many people these days. We've tossed out values to go play and be little kids again. Many of us baby boomers are the most insatiable, immature group of people.

We don't want to work hard to build anything with value...what's that about? The only thing we want to work hard for is to get that boat or nice car, or to go to Hawaii. We don't have the internal fortitude to make a lasting relationship work. We neglect human beings and take better care of our cars, homes, boats and other toys. I liked what John Travolta stated in his interview in Good housekeeping of July 2000, pg. 177. He said he and his wife decided that it would be for "better or for worse," and that if they could stay for the better part, then they had to stick it out for the worse too. They are in it "until the end." I admire that man; he's what you would call a *real* man in every sense of the word, and his wife is a *real* woman in every sense as well. *They've grown up,* they play*, and* they work. They know they'll have rough times, but they're going to go through them...period!

The thing that scares us is we just never know what rough times will look like. So, when they do appear, we're stunned and caught off-guard. We say things like, "No, my God, this can't be who he/she is."

"Worse" can come in so many ways, and it's always a surprise no matter what. So, my advice: "Stick it out." Get to the deeper part of the intimacy and the reward, after all the B.S., will be so incredible it will have been worth it. The problem is no one wants to wait that long and go through all the muck and mire to get to the gold. But to have the gold, you have to go through the garbage...*there is no other way!*

What has happened to us? I personally think that we've lost our strength of character, our ability to stick things out for the long haul. We are wimpy, selfish, and insatiable adults. How does that nonsense look to our children? I know it must sicken them to see us go from one relationship to another! I know what you're thinking right now; you're defending your immoral choices by blaming the other person instead of looking at yourself. Instead, you say things like, "Well, Joe didn't work; he just wasn't thoughtful enough. Oh, and the one with Frank didn't work either; he was just a selfish bastard. I just pick the wrong men every time!"

May I ask you something? *Why the hell didn't you just date the man and find that out? Why did you have to move in and drag your kids into it to find out things you wouldn't like about him?* You men...you go from one relationship to another because you just can't find that "perfect" woman. You know...the one that has the perfect figure, the one who always looks beautiful, cooks, cleans, has sex with you every night, *never* complains, is always polite, and has no needs whatsoever. And when she doesn't meet all of *your* needs, you look for every little flaw she might have, and then rationalize that she's just not the one for you—so you break her heart and just like Peter Pan, you're off to the next adventure—ever searching for perfection—completely forgetting that *you* are far from perfect! How pathetically *narcissistic* of you.

A wise old woman I met in passing said something to me that I have never forgotten. When I complained that I just couldn't find the "right" man, she replied with something deeply profound. "Anne, it isn't about finding the right person...it's about *being* the right person, never forget that." I haven't to this day.

Listen to me carefully. All your relationships are going to end until you learn to *be* the right person, *and that takes work...PERIOD!*

If you're married, just stick it out (unless there's physical abuse, continuous drug/alcohol abuse, or continuous affairs). If you're shacking up, get an apartment or something by yourself and take a look at who you *really* are, then clean up your act, date respectfully, wait for a decent man that will ask you to marry him and when he does, for God's sake say yes! Then stick it out for the long haul—if you're mature enough, that is!

Shacking Up Is

#32 UNDIGNIFIED

UNDIGNIFIED
Lacking in elevation of character or worthiness.

L et's look at the word dignity and what it means in the positive. Dignity: *"Bearing conduct of manner indicative of self respect, elevation of character worthiness."* So, let me now ask you this: how's your conduct, hmm? Is it indicative of dignity? I'll tell you right now that the guy you're living with is lovin' every minute of his free-for-all situation with you. He's not worried the least little bit about your dignity or his for that matter. In fact, he's as content as a bear is with a beehive full of honey. But you, on the other hand, while shacking up with your buddy, feel things like...anxiety...sex...fear...sex...confusion...sex...dread...sex...uncertainty, well, you get the drift, right?

Your gut feelings aren't lying to you. You're the one who's gettin' screwed (no pun intended), and you don't even know it! He has no problems at all with the situation, because in today's society, or at any time in history for that matter, the man never looks like a "slut" or "loose." Even though we'd like to *think* we've "come so far," I've got news for you...we're still living in the day and age where the underlying current (if not said to your face or in words) is that you're either loose or slutty for what you're doing.

No self-respecting man will really ever marry you. I know right about now that your brain is panicking; that sinking feeling in your heart has just returned after you worked so hard to make it go away. I don't care what he says to you, you're being used and you know it.

Just do two things: watch his actions, then listen to his words. That's how you'll know he's full of crap!

So now ask yourself one more time, "Do I have any dignity?" If the answer is *no,* you'd better go down to your nearest grocery store, get yourself some boxes, and then line up a mover, because the winds of change are a blowin'.

Hey, and if you still don't think I know what I'm talking about—and if you've been with him for any length of time—here's a little test you can do on your little shack-up honey. Go up to him and say, "Honey, I love you. When do you think we can set a date to get married?" If you asked him while he was eating, did he choke violently? Did he quickly change the subject? Did he laugh and say, "Ah, honey, we've only been living together for six years. We need at least a few more years to get to know each other *really* well before we do *that!*" Or, if he completely ignores you, you're in *big* trouble, sweetie; he's not in the least bit interested. So *please,* think hard about what you really want…because he sure as hell isn't!

Shacking Up Is

#33 UNHEALTHY

UNHEALTHY
Harmful to good health...morally harmful.

Crying, heart palpations, worry, anxiety, fear, anger, headaches, stomach problems, more crying, confusion, sleepless nights, missing work due to shacking up relationship problems the night before, more crying. Hey, I know a lot of you out there have gone through this; I'm certainly not the only one. I think the reason why this happens is because the men in the relationship don't want marriage and put us off, and it causes a great deal of anxiety for us women.

The anxiety we experience has started a lot of fights, and it's much more upsetting to us women than it is to you men. But what do you expect? A man who knows that a woman does not care about compromising her worth will compromise it right along with her. He has nothing to lose, remember, he's not going to be looked upon as slutty. She is not as valued as a woman that holds out until marriage. If he doesn't want to wait, he doesn't care about you one iota!

Shacking up is a health hazard. Let me name some things that you feel, and I don't even know you. There is no sense of well-being, there's always deep anxiety, and anger is there at some level as well. You feel suspicious of him and his motives (because he puts you off all the time about a commitment). Dread is a familiar friend too. You have no sense of finality. It causes an erratic change in your blood pressure; I have felt it throughout my shacking up lifestyle and it's very uncomfortable. It's caused from all the crying because I knew I was the one, and the only one, who looked slutty. I knew everyone was looking at me and shaking their heads. The humiliation was more than I could bear, but my humiliation was of no concern to him.

It seemed like he didn't think one single, solitary minute about how bad he was hurting me or how much pain I was in. He simply didn't act like he cared. I'd see this grin on his face when he'd say, "Ahh, honey, you know I love you…" *Just not quite enough to marry me,* I'd think. He was not concerned about how bad my chest hurt from the pressure of the uncertainty I felt. (Hey, why should he get married? Why buy the cow when you can get the milk for free?) He never once consoled me. Never, did he ever come into the room where I was crying and say, "I am so sorry for the pain I'm causing you by not marrying you." Not once!

I could go on, but do I need to? You know I'm right, and it feels really sickening, doesn't it? Doesn't it make you want to do something right about now…like move out? Don't you feel used, confused, angry, foolish, embarrassed, cheap, disgusted, and sad?

Come on; listen to me. I'm the example of what *not* to be. If you learn anything, learn from me what not to do. So, get health back in your life. Acute stress caused by shacking up together is detrimental to your health, and if it lasts for a long period of time, it not only ages you but can cause serious health problems. Compromising your worth is not good for your health or the health of your children. When the stress of living together doesn't seem to be so bad at different times, I have to tell you from my own experience that there's always a subtle stress level taking place, which erodes away at your health. I know you feel it. Is he really worth all that?

If our children know better than we do, then we need to take a serious look at ourselves and rearrange our pathetic lives before it's too late. On the side of a pack of cigarettes it reads: "The surgeon general warns that cigarette smoking can be hazardous to your health." Well, my warning will be a lifestyle warning, and it will be on the bumper of my car: WARNING: SHACKING UP CAN BE HAZARDOUS TO YOUR HEALTH!

Shacking Up Is

#34 UNNERVING

UNNERVING
To deprive of courage, strength, or determination.

As I was scanning the dictionary for words I could use to identify my lifestyle, I came upon the word unnerving. It says in the definition: *"To deprive of courage, strength, or determination."*

I have learned that it's *after* you're in the relationship, and you've gotten so deeply involved, that when you do finally come to your senses, you have a difficult time getting the courage to say, "I'm moving out unless we get married."

You *don't* say it because you know the answer he's going to give you will go something like this: "Go ahead. You don't have any shackles on. No one's holding you here." Your heart sinks to the ground! That's not what you wanted to hear from someone who supposedly loves you. Now you *know* he doesn't love you like you love him. Everything is based on a one-sided affair...your side. You're in love all by yourself.

Courage, strength, and determination fly out the window, taking your heart with them because now you know you have to put up a wall of protection against the uncertain future you have with this person.

You quickly pretend that you didn't hear what he said and go on your usual way, pretending that everything is okay. But you know in your guts, you're living a lie.

Here is what shacking up will offer you. First, when you put up that barrier (which you have every reason to) a few things happen. A psychological wall is built, which in turn puts the brakes on for true intimacy, which in turn makes your relationship fake. That's as far as it's going to go. Sound like something you'll settle for?

Secondly, trust is lost because of the wall you have to put up so that your heart doesn't break so badly you can't function later when a parting of ways does occur. The fact of the matter is, you don't know where this person is coming from.

Third, when you're not married, it's *NO HOLDS BARRED*—anything can happen. It's open for them to come and go as they please. With no marriage, they have a variety of options open to them. No commitment, no conscience, it's that simple…and oh, don't let me forget easy, too, just like a baby boomer likes it! I need to add something here to the children of baby boomers—don't fall into the same trap your parents are in, please. Watch and for God's sake learn from them and the mess they've made of their lives.

My reason for mentioning baby boomers is because we seem to have started this trashy trend of shacking up. *Shame on us, is all I have to say.*

To sum everything up, when you're in a shack-up situation, it becomes unnerving. You will lose all courage, strength, and determination to tell him/her (mostly him) that you want to be married or that you need to move out if they don't want to be married. Then when the cold, hard words are spoken…"Nope, I don't want to get married." Even then, when they say it so blatantly, you won't muster up the strength, determination, and courage to leave (or have them leave if that's the case) because you've invested time and emotions. It's more painful to think about leaving than it is to stay, in spite of their cold, heartless, uncaring answer.

As I said before, when you choose this lifestyle, it's almost always a one-sided affair; usually, the woman is having it all by herself. However, I will say that I'm sure that every so often, a man wants to get married and the woman doesn't, so I will write this for the men who are in that position.

Now with that…go gather some courage, strength, and determination and move out. It will hurt at first, but in the long run, you will feel strong, you will have acquired more courage, and you'll be able to choose someone with guts and morals. It's worth the wait!

This last little comment was made by my now deceased mother. She said, "Anne, I'd rather be alone than in hell shacking up with a man." Thank you, Mom, wherever you are right now. I love you!

Shacking Up Is

#35 UNPROTECTED

UNPROTECTED
To allow attack, to allow loss, to not shield.

Imagine you're looking out of the window. Your children are throwing a ball in the front yard when one of them accidentally throws it into the direction of a busy street. The older one runs to the edge of the sidewalk (you see him eyeing the street for safety, or lack thereof), preparing to run into the street and retrieve the object of his enjoyment for the day. His foot makes the step into the thoroughfare; he *has* to get his ball. You see a car speeding down the road.

You bolt out the door and yell, "Stop!" Your heart is racing so fast it makes your head spin. You run and grab the child up. That was a close call! What if you hadn't been near the window? Your child could have been seriously injured.

It can be so frightening when our children get into scary situations. It makes us feel vulnerable that they could be so unprotected at times when we're not there, and there's nothing we can do about it.

Well, I have to be the first to tell you that shacking up with someone leaves your children unprotected. Lowering your standards steals your children's protection from the outside world. Don't they deserve to be protected until they're old enough to fend for themselves? My God, they depend on you! Even animals know how to take better care of their babies than we do! Why are we like this when we know that human babies are the most vulnerable creatures? It just baffles me!

157

Shacking up leaves your children open to people who aren't their father or mother, and the situation can be so heart-wrenching. I'll tell you of an experience I had when my children were small.

We knew a couple whose children were friends with my children. They were shacking up. He had a boy from a previous marriage, and she had none. At one point in time, I saw a terrible display of cruelty …I was taken so off-guard I didn't even know how to respond. This woman was cruel to his boy; she intimidated, screamed at, and scared him so bad that I felt despair for him. God only knows how often this had happened. I would find out later the result of her abuse towards him. I sent this chapter to the prison, where he resides at this time, and told him I knew what had happened to him and how very sorry I was that he'd had to live that way. The day I saw this display of terror, I had to pick up some artwork she had for me. The boy walked in from school shortly after I arrived. He wasn't greeted with a, "Hi, sweetie, how was your day at school?" Oh no, he was screamed at viciously to go to his room!

He was on restriction for "something" he had done…of course! He obeyed and was careful not to slam his door shut too hard, lest he be punished more severely.

After an hour had gone by, she screamed his name. When he didn't answer, she stomped down the hall to his door and *kicked* it opened! I stood there, stunned at this sort of behavior; I could barely believe that she would do that in front of me. She looked around the room but he was nowhere to be found. She left to go hunt for him.

She could not figure out how he had gotten out of his room without her seeing him. She went to other parts of the house. I stayed in the room. I had a hunch. Above the rather tall closet were two small sliding doors. I walked over to them and, standing on my toes, I reached up and slid one of the doors open. What I saw broke my heart…There he was, curled up in a ball, sweating profusely from being confined for so long. The fear I saw on his face is forever etched in my mind.

She never imagined that he would be able to get up that high, and so she thought he had left the house. I smiled at him, and he smiled back—a sad smile. I put my finger to my lips and mouthed, "Shh," he nodded a "yes" back. I closed the door and walked out of the room, never mentioning that he was there.

I'm sure that she had always been mean and short with him. She treated her animals just as mean. Her language was like that of a drunken sailor; every sentence was splashed with F this and F that. The last time I ever remember talking to that woman was when she called and said, "I'm sending him to F-ing juvenile hall!" (Get that. He's not even her child, but she was going to send him to juvenile hall!) What Chutzpah! I often wondered if the dad saw this display of emotional violence being perpetrated against his son. My guess was she didn't do it in front of him.

I intervened. "If he's that much of a problem," I told her, "we'll take him off your hands."

"No!" she yelled. "He's going to F-ing juvenile hall. That's where he F-ing belongs."

"Look," I said emphatically. "He doesn't need to go to juvenile hall. He'll be destroyed there. He can stay with us."

"No, he's going. That's where he F-ing deserves to go!" she said angrily.

The sad thing about all of it was...*he was only nine years old!*

To this day, I have not forgotten the suffering that that little boy up in the closet went through—all because his parent left him unprotected. I will never forget him! In fact, this chapter is dedicated to him. My family has not forgotten you.

The suffering he endured by that cruel woman is too unthinkable to contemplate. He endured years of fear and dread from some tyrant that wasn't even his mother!

As you know, this is just one story out of thousands where children are left unprotected when their parent is away, and they are left with the *unparent.* They are left to be abused, treated scornfully, molested, and sometimes the extreme...murdered. As you know, many of these children, especially the boys that are in this kind environment, usually end up doing jail time or worse—prison. In almost all cases, you will find that they were victims of abuse when they were children. Let's face it, do you know whether the person you're shacking up with might be doing the same thing to your child without your knowledge? The bottom line is...*you don't know.* Were you aware that the statistics for molestation of children when people just shack up with someone is higher than with people who are married? Think about that before you decide to make such a deadly move.

Please remember that shacking up leaves your children (and yourself) unprotected. I know that you're too smart to let your child be exposed to that kind of evil. Unprotected means to allow attack, to allow loss, to not shield. There's nothing worse than being too little to protect yourself against a person such as the woman in this story.

Start now and protect yourself and your children. Do the right thing and move out. Shacking up leaves you vulnerable and unprotected!

Shacking Up Is

#36 UNSANCTIFIED

UNSANCTIFIED

No sacredness or hallowed character, no holiness, no saintliness, no godliness.

Wow! That definition sure is a mouthful, if I do say so myself. Does it make you feel crappy about shacking up? Well, it's supposed to, so there. When I reread Webster's definition, I couldn't help but again think of the Cleaver family. June and Ward Cleaver... now that's a family that we need to emulate. They had what it takes: guts and no fear. I don't care if it was a TV show...so what? It was written by people who liked that kind of life and tried to portray it by making up this little family that *all* of America loved and wanted to be like.

We can be like them if we really want to, but it takes work. What has happened between then, when "The Beaver" was on, and now that we just no longer care about holiness, saintliness, and godliness?

You know what the truth is? We just plain don't have the guts or backbone. In fact, I know that some of you are sarcastically saying, "Oh, yeah, I want to be just like them...ha." I ask you, why can't we be like them? Remember how much we liked the show? How good it felt each time we would sit down and watch it? We *can* be like that; it's only a thought away. Ask Anthony Robins, the motivational speaker—he'll tell you! We were born with the capacity to create just about anything we want. We *can* create a wonderful marriage and make it *stay* wonderful by lots and lots of hard work. Anything with value takes hard work! But that work includes *you* too. You can't expect the other person to do it all by themselves. If you *both* do the work together, a good marriage *will* happen!

What has made us just not care about how shacking up looks to our children and loved ones, as well as others who aren't necessarily close to us? It's all so sad, to say the least. I don't know about you, but I miss the good and simple life "Leave it to Beaver" offered. Looking back, I can honestly say that I had a family a lot like the "Cleaver" family. I miss it so much. I ache to be back there. So why can't we work on doing the right thing? What's so wrong with it? I know…it gets in the way of your very comfortable setup, right?

Well now, we're so glad *you're* comfortable, forget anyone else around you and whether they feel comfortable being around you while you're shacking up with someone. You just don't give a damn about what anyone else thinks. Just as long as you're comfy, that's what counts. *Pacifier anyone?*

The bottom line is you don't trust yourself to be married and stay married. You don't want to be locked into a lifetime with that one person and all of his/her flaws and annoying little habits. Of course, you don't have any annoying habits worth mentioning, and if you *did* recognize any of the few you think have…well, they're just not as bad as his/hers. I know!

Let's face it, you don't have the endurance or patience, or anything else it takes for that matter, to make a marriage work. You still like being spoon-fed, and you also think it's up to the other person to make you happy. If he or she fails, well, you'll just move out and find someone else with whom to start another shack-up arrangement. That's so much easier; blaming someone else is the ticket! You'll never look at yourself and realize that it's just as much you as the other person. So why don't you just *grow up* and get a *real* life? Preferably one with a little sanctity in it. You know why you go from one relationship to another? Because you're scared to death of *true* intimacy, and that's what I think the real reason is for all the shacking up we're doing. True intimacy is *HARD…REALLY HARD!*

We've lowered our standards and have gone the way of the fool, but remember, my fellow baby boomers—and the rest of you that are out there shacking up—time is speeding up, as you are well aware. I ask you, are you going to sacrifice your holiness, your saintliness, and your godliness right now for something fast and cheap?

Listen to me, I'm still having a really hard time seeing the despicable way we're living when there are so many avenues we can access to help ourselves—seminars, books, tapes, you name it, it's out there to help us. *Hello, are you hearing me? We're still screwing up!*

Soon, you'll pay—when you're old, alone, and you don't have a mate (because you went through them like water, and finally you gave up because you always thought it was the other person causing all the problems...how delusional on your part, I might add). Your children aren't anywhere to be found (they simply don't give a damn now because hey, they remember a time when you didn't care about them). Now what? That's a scary thought. I've sat for a long time thinking about it myself.

Okay, straight up: when you compromise your sanctity and you women give your bodies away for free (men rather like giving their bodies away for free so this does not apply to them), when you don't care about your children, if you have any, then you are going to pay the ultimate price.

You men, it's time for your flogging. If you're shacking up and you have sons, you're a horrible example to them on how to treat women! They are going to emulate *you*. If you act like it's no big deal, they will treat the women in their lives like they're no big deal. They're going to emulate you whether you like it or not. Think about the golden rule: treat others as you would want others to treat you. If that saying is too "girlie" for the men that might be reading this book, here's another one: karma will kick you in your butt! So, walk with trepidation! (In case you don't know what that means, here's the definition: *"Fearful anxiety."*)

Don't you feel even remotely embarrassed shacking up with someone in front of your children? Why would you invite a perfect stranger (to the children) into your home and have sex with him or her in the other room, *JUST BECAUSE THE DOOR IS CLOSED!?* Your children understand what's going on; they're not stupid or ignorant.

I was so embarrassed for my children to even suspect what I was doing the first few months that I was shacking up. When I would put my children to bed, I would wait until they were asleep, *then* I would go to bed. Rest never came easy because I always felt stressed out about shacking up with the person. I would also worry about waking up in time so they wouldn't know I was sleeping with my shack-up lover. But, of course, that didn't work because sometimes I overslept and my children would knock on the door, at which time I would tell my lover to get on the floor where there was a bed ready made—for just such an emergency. That way, my children would not think I was sleeping with him. How insane I was to think I could get away with that!

When I look back on it now, I feel so sick inside. I feel agony for my sweet children. I was so stupid, that's for sure. All those years of holiness I lived as a devout Christian, married to a man who was faithful to me, who worked hard, and who was an awesome father to the three incredible children we had together...*vanished in the blink of an unholy eye.*

Sad, but it's the ugly truth. I can never repair the damage that has been unleashed upon my helpless children, and my now ex-husband, by my own hand. When I do think back, I just sink into depression over it because I can *never* take it back. I can never heal the pain I caused my children through my immoral living.

Listen, don't do *anything* you can't take back...*please, I implore you.* I told my sons that I would turn what I did into something that hopefully wakes up others and gets people turned back in the right direction. Please...think about this. You're worth the very best, aren't you? Think deeply for a moment. What do you think godliness feels like? What do you think holiness feels like? What do you think a hallowed character feels like? Consider this for a while before you read the rest of this book.

Work on getting those feelings back. Don't lower your standards for some fast pleasure. It may be fun at the moment, but it brings about a deadly result in the end. Feeling wholesome and godly feels a lot better than feeling cheap and crappy about what you're doing right now, doesn't it? If you work on feeling wholesome and godly, it will automatically spill over to your children, and then maybe they can start to feel safe and protected once again.

If you don't have children, and you're single and shacking up, do the right thing...move out! You start the example, others will follow suit. After all, someone started shacking up a long time ago, and he or she had a friend who saw them doing it that thought, *Hey, I'm going to do it.* And then a friend saw *them* do it, and they thought,

I'm going to do it too! That's how it starts. So, reverse the trend. *Don't shack up!*

So with all that I have said, let me ask you this: do you feel holy, sacred, saintly, and godly while you're shacking up? Close your eyes right now. Go back to when you were a child. Pick out a favorite memory from when you were about five or six. Feel your innocence then. Doesn't it feel wonderful? You were untarnished then by your blunders and bad decisions. Now, bring yourself to the present...*yuck* is all you have to say, I'm sure of that. You can change it.

Do it now...right this very minute. Don't hesitate! Make it a rule. NO SHACKING UP.

Shacking Up Is

#37 UNSETTLING

UNSETTLED

Not fixed or stable, not determined, undecided.

U nsettled is not a good feeling! Have you ever moved more than once in a year? Just thinking about it makes me tired. All that hard work only to do it again? All I have to say to that is…ugh. I can't even think of it for long without wanting to take a nap!

It says in the dictionary that unsettled means *"not fixed or stable."* It also defines the word unsettled as *"not determined"* and *"undecided."* Isn't that a precarious way for you to live? Kind of like you always have to expect at some point to move again, and the thought is overwhelming. You always have that feeling deep inside of you that says your relationship won't be permanent, and it makes you feel really…well…unsettled?

I also looked up the word precarious and it's a good word to describe shacking up. It means: *"Dependent on circumstances beyond one's control, uncertain."* It even goes so far as to say dangerous because it's insecure and unsteady!

You've probably thought about things like, *What if this doesn't work?* (Because you already know the chances are not high that it will.) *Where am I going to go next?* Thoughts like, *God, I can't move again; it will just take too much out of me. I'll have to put my stuff back into storage again. I don't want to start another relationship, I'm forty-four years old!* You feel scared and depressed. Oh, I know those feelings well, my friend. So I ask you, do you want this for yourself?

171

Is this how you really want to live? You know that when you have a mate that is on the same page as you, you both have common interests, you both nurture the other, you both watch out for the other, and you work things out when you have disagreements. You're careful not to purposely hurt the other. There's stability in that and you know it, but that takes time and patience and that's something we adults don't seem to have the ability to exercise.

*Marriage is only as stable as the two people in it (*always keep in mind that you're one of the people). If you take your time to know someone before you get married, and you can see (notice I didn't put feel) that he's/she's going to be reliable (and there are men/women out there that are very reliable), then you can make plans for the rest of your life and feel very secure and settled.

A man/woman that loves you wants nothing more than for you to feel settled with him/her. If he/she isn't concerned about whether or not you are, then you know that person is not for you.

If you're a woman and shacking up, it's very hard for you to keep your emotions out of it after you have sex, and that's a fact! Because the minute you sleep with your honey bumpkins you might as well throw your common sense to the wind!

Ahh…to be settled is such a cozy feeling. Wouldn't you agree? I used to feel it, when I was married the first time and doing the right thing. I have never felt it since that time. I long for it so much, but I will never have it completely because I forfeited it when I broke up my marriage.

Shacking up is very unsettling, and if you want to feel that feeling every day that's up to you, but I would hope you're smarter than that and that you value yourself and your children more than having a man/woman move in and keep you company. Cozy and shacking up don't go together, and neither do you and your shack-up honey.

So, either face reality and move out or have them move out—or look at each other and say you want to do the right thing, and get married. There should be no problem if you both really love each other, right? Then what's to stop you?

If you both don't want to get married then it's all a sham, and you're just using each other. Worst of all, you're hurting any children that might be involved. I know you don't want to do that, do you? Think about it, and make changes right now; you owe it to your children, and if you don't have children, you owe it to your family members, friends, and society to do the right thing.

Shacking Up Is

#38 UNTRUSTWORTHY

UNTRUSTWORTHY
Unreliable.

Do you believe and feel right at this moment, while you're shacking up, that you have complete trust in your partner? Think for just a moment. If you answered, "Yes" to that question, then you deserve all the heartache you'll get. I hate to say it, but it's true. Just the very act of shacking up denotes untrustworthiness.

You and I both know that there can't be real, *true* trust in the shacking up lifestyle. I can vouch for that, and I even had a ring! I had to actually force a date out of him after years! *Force*—did you read that? (I'll bet you can see the beads of sweat on my forehead from where you're at.) It seemed he just flat out didn't love me enough to want to give me a date. So you think I should feel trust' after all this time? *Bottom line*...I didn't.

Untrustworthy means unreliable, so of course I had to look that up in the dictionary as well, and it's pretty unsettling if you ask me. Here's the definition: *"Irresponsible, disreputable, dishonest, undependable, questionable, conniving, guileless, deceitful."* Now, after reading those definitions, do you still feel the same way about your "roommate?" When I read them, it made me feel even *more* upset and frustrated than I'd felt before about shacking up with someone I had known for only three months of my entire life. I can't believe that I put that amount of trust in someone I didn't even know! What in God's name was I thinking? Honestly speaking, I wasn't. I went with the moment, and I listened to all the nice things he said.

177

There was a lot of arguing and some fun, but I wasn't thinking the whole time.

Now, I want you to look at each of the words in the definition for unreliable. Say each one out loud slowly. Do any one of them feel even remotely true? If so, please help yourself and do the right thing: leave that situation. If you stay in your live in situation just know this: the odds are against you.

Isn't it a lot easier to meet someone and date for a few years, and get to know their personality and character with all their good points *and* all of their flaws? Then you can make an intellectual decision based not on sex and emotions, but on your brain and experiences to know whether someone might be good for you or not in the long haul.

Lastly, sex is a wonderful thing, but it will cloud your decision-making ability and cause you a lot of pain in the long run. Keep sex out of the relationship until you know that person is the one for you. I know in this day and age this is almost impossible for people to do, sex is a very powerful urge, but the wait will be well worth it, and the trust and contentment you will feel because you did will far outweigh not having had sex for that period of time.

Shacking Up Is

#39 WORTHLESS

WORTHLESS
Without value, valueless.

Worthlessness...now that's a feeling everyone should have every so often, wouldn't you agree? Well, I don't think any of us want to wake up feeling totally worthless. I must tell you though, because of my immoral choices, I have had my dose of waking up with it. Feeling worthless was self-induced by the despicable, selfish choices I made in my sad little existence at the time.

I can hear what you're thinking..."Well, that's you...*NOT* me." Oh come on, you think you're different from the rest of the humans on this planet? You think I don't know that when you're alone, the fact that you're shacking up with someone eats at you? And when your head hits that pillow at night, you rest easy? I can tell you this, if you're in bed right now and you're reading this book, look over to your little shugee pie. Does he look troubled? Hell no! He's sleeping like a baby, huh? You're the one reading the book...I rest my case.

I got news for you: you're just like everyone else, taking what you can, and you don't care whom you mow down while doing it. You don't even think about the consequences. You ignore your children's feelings about it; you don't even remotely *care* what they think! If you don't have children, again, think about your family, your mom and dad, your grandparents, your siblings...they *do* have feelings about it, whether you like it or not. Most of them are just polite to your face. I'm sorry, I know that I've said this before, but I just want

181

to make sure you're hearing me. Sorry to rain on your parade, but it's the truth. *You've* put them in an uncomfortable position, so don't expect them to like it!

I can feel you getting angry right about now. You're probably thinking, *Well, who the hell are you to tell me how to live? It's none of your damn business.*

Well, I've got something to say: we're all interwoven, with each affecting the other, and if you don't know this, then you're blind to how the universe is set up. You need to get some books on the subject to help you see a bigger picture than what your seeing. We are all in a very delicate balancing act in this world and we all need to start being more kind to one another and a lot more wiser for starters. Now, getting mad at me for speaking the truth isn't going to fix your problem.

Shacking up is a worthless thing to do. It doesn't bring honor to your children (if you have any), and it's certainly not character building. We've thrown character out and replaced it with worthless shacking up because we want things to come easy to us. We're spoiled little brats who want instant gratification, and so we compromise our worth. Sad...but oh so very true. So, if you like feeling worthless, just keep doing what you're doing. You'll eventually reach total worthlessness—that's when your life will really get out of control, like mine did. Remember, worthlessness means without value. Get value back in your life by doing the right thing, and that is to *not* shack up. Shacking up with someone steals your value and self-worth, so just don't do it!

Shacking Up Is

#40 LOVE IS NOT ENOUGH!

LOVE
A profoundly tender passionate affection for another person.

W ell, now that's all nice and mushy, I know. I also know that the feelings of love towards someone after sex (mostly for women) can obscure your good judgment towards that person. That's a fact! Hopping in bed with your would-be lover will definitely throw reason and sensibility out the window. *I* know; *I'm* living proof of clouded judgment.

There were signs along the way. I'm not talking little signs... these were big, blatant signs that I just chose to *blatantly* ignore, and because I had sex with him it was really difficult to see what was necessary to make a proper decision about the relationship. My emotions kept me there, not my sensibility.

The longer you shack up, the harder it will be to leave. I did fall in love with my honey bunches, but I'm not saying that it automatically meant it was good for my well-being...because it wasn't. (Re-read the section, An Emotional Roller Coaster Ride.)

So, you think that love is enough to make you stay together? Well, love to you and love to most men is not the same. You see, men can have sex and walk away unscathed. Women, on the other hand, well, we're not so lucky that way. The minute we have sex, it's all over. Our emotions come spilling out and our hearts take over. That's when clouded judgment rules our life, and it can take years for us to come to our senses—but not before a lot of pain, heartache, tears, yelling, and confusion. (There's no need to say more; I know you understand all too well what I'm talking about.)

As I said, love is not enough to keep two people together. So let's talk about that right now. Other than love, what makes for a lasting relationship? For starters, mutual respect for each other. I looked up the word respect because I like to know the exact definitions of words, so there's no misinterpretation by anyone.

So, respect's definition is as follows: *"Proper courtesy. The condition of being esteemed, to hold in esteem."* So, I looked up the word esteem. Looking up the words builds a clear picture of the points I'm making. Here's what it says: *"To regard with respect or admiration."* Now, let's look up the word admiration: *"To regard with pleasure, approval, and often wonder; to regard highly, respect."*

Now ask yourself if that's how you're being treated. A person who loves you will treat you the way he/she would treat themselves— with respect, honor, kindness, tenderness, thoughtfulness, and consideration. Are you being treated that way? You might say right about now, "Well, Anne, everyone can't be that way one hundred percent of the time; we're human," and I won't argue with that. We will slip up if we've had a bad day, or if (for us women) it's that time of the month, or if we've been sitting in stopped traffic for two hours and we're late for a doctor's appointment. I know these things.

Though if (to your undoing) you end up shacking up together, and then you start seeing a consistent negative pattern of behavior because he doesn't respect you for moving in and giving yourself away for nothing, and you let inertia take over to avoid the truth that you're in the wrong place, you will lead a life of anguish. When you face the truth—that he does not hold your peace of mind close to his heart and it's shown by the things that he says and does or *doesn't do*—if you continue *not* to believe that how he's treating you is conducive to your well-being, then he will continue to act towards you the way he does, simply because he knows you'll stay no matter what.

Love is not enough to keep two people together. You have to share the same value system. If you value marriage and he doesn't, then it's time to leave.

I pray for each and every person that struggles with this extremely important issue. It's easier said than done. Get the courage, because life is short and getting shorter by the minute. There's no time to waste.

This last paragraph is for my three sons, David, Jacob, and Isaiah. I want the readers of this book to bear witness right now. I am deeply remorseful for my immoral lifestyle and how it affected you. Whatever shame, tears, or pain it brought to you, will you forgive me for it?

I consider myself blessed beyond measure for having you three incredible souls in my life. Thank you for all you are and for all you have been to me. You have been my light when my life was at its darkest. You tolerated me and my despicable choices, and yet you loved me unconditionally. *You* are what every human should strive to be. This book is dedicated to you, and it's *for you*...from me. I love you.

Now, for those who have just read this...go and find *your* children, and ask them to forgive you too. If you don't have children, go to those people you know who are probably offended by what you're doing (Grandma and Grandpa for instance), and ask them to forgive you. Start right now to get morality back into your life because IT'S TIME TO STOP SHACKING UP!

AN IMPORTANT MESSAGE FROM ANNE'S HUSBAND

I'd like to tell all you men and women out there that I firmly believe in the institution of marriage. "Shacking up" or cohabiting before marriage is neither intimate nor romantic. How can it be? It's really just playing house, and wanting all the benefits without the obligations. So what usually happens when it "doesn't work out" after she's already given her mind, body, and soul in the fake home? She winds up in an emotional tizzy with her heart broken. Her hopes and dreams are shattered because she could never discover his true intentions—and we all know the old cliché, "The road to hell is paved with good intentions."

There is no doubt in my mind that a man, if he truly loves and respects his woman, will ask her to marry him much quicker if she doesn't "move in."

The commitment to marriage changes everything. Your way of thinking becomes more clear, and the connection is real, not fake.

I almost lost my beautiful wife because I was one of those "get to know you" and "I'm not ready" kind of thinkers. What was I saying? What did I mean? What was I thinking? I love Anne but I wasn't ready? I had to re-think this through. I really didn't even know what I meant with those words. I was letting my male nature control me, instead of me controlling it. Anne was always right, and I knew she truly loved me. Marriage was the right thing to do.

Sometimes, it's just really difficult for us men to come to grips with our male nature. Let's be honest guys, it's not natural for a man to want to commit himself to one woman. We're visual. We can look at a pair of legs on a billboard sign, and it grabs our attention...we want to conquer it for ourselves. It's only a pair of legs! So why does it stimulate us?

Our problem is that we have the innate urge to inseminate everything that walks. That's the animal part of us. That's why we fear commitment so much. To elevate ourselves as humans, we have to get that wild, animal nature that controls us, *under control.* That's why commitment is so difficult for us men. We would like to have all the perks and the freedom without the commitment, and we'll believe our own lines to get them. We may even delude ourselves into believing that we mean well...because when we act like we mean well, it appeals to a woman's emotions. Once we have her emotions tied up by seducing her with lines that *we* believe...asking her to move in is a breeze. Now that she has allowed herself to be seduced, we know more than likely she'll say "yes." After all, she gave us what we wanted! She said "yes," hoping that in the near future she'll get a ring and a date.

Now I've run across more women these days who say, "I don't need a ring and a date. I'm fine with just "living together." I'd love to address that statement. First of all, you're deluding yourself as much as we men delude ourselves into believing we mean well. The very fact that you moved in shows you have no self-respect. So, you'll just settle and convince yourself that you don't need that very important commitment of a ring and a date. Why are those things so important? As Anne puts it in her Frequently Asked Questions, the fact that a man wears his ring everyday shows the world he's in love with that person, is committed only to her, and is proud of that commitment. That's why having a ring and a date is so important, because you *know* where his loyalty lies. You also know how he *really* feels towards you. When you just shack up, because you women are emotional creatures, after a certain amount of time you become uneasy about his intentions. Ladies, just do yourself a favor and say no when your man asks you to move in, unless, of course, you don't mind being robbed of your soul and valuable time.

"But honey schnook-ums, I'm not ready." Now there's an original line. Who do we think we're kidding? And what do we mean by, "I'm not ready?" Let's be honest. I'm not ready means, "I'm not ready to commit to *you!!*"

Still want to play house? Still want to avoid true intimacy? Still want to lower your standards for an elusive goal where the odds of staying together (even if you do finally get married) are against you? Why would you accept less than the ideal of marriage by giving up your mind, body, and soul without commitment? Have we become a better society by knowing almost five million people are shacking up? The sad truth is, we are *not* better. In fact, we are worse.

Information from *The National Marriage Project* at Rutgers University came up with three warnings why living together outside of marriage may not be a good idea. The statistics also coincide with a *USA Today* study in the July 28, 2000 issue. Again, this article is based on information from *The National Marriage Project*.

1. Higher Divorce Rate

Perhaps the most compelling and widespread argument against living together before marriage is that several researchers say it increases the risk of breaking up. Virtually all studies of this topic have shown that the chance of divorce is significantly greater for married couples who lived together first. And in 1992, the National Survey of Families and Households found that, in 3,300 families, married couples who had lived together first were judged to be 46 percent more likely to get divorced.

2. Lower Quality of Life

When it comes to living together, more research suggests that the quality of life for unmarried couples is far lower than for married couples. Researchers David Popenoe and Barbara Dafoe Whitehead say cohabiting couples report lower levels of happiness, lower levels of sexual exclusivity and sexual satisfaction, and poorer relationships with their parents. Annual rates of depression are more than three times higher. And, finally, cohabiting women are more likely than married women to suffer physical and sexual abuse.

3. Living Together Doesn't Necessarily Lead to Marriage

After five to seven years, 21 percent of most cohabiting couples are still doing just that—cohabiting, without getting married. In a new study by Popenoe and Whitehead, one of the top 10 reasons why men said they are reluctant to get married at all is because they can simply live with a woman—and enjoy the same benefits.

So, there you have it. As a man, I've laid all my cards on the table. I have personally experienced the negative effects of what shacking up can do to a relationship. It's just not a good thing to do as outlined in the *40 Reasons Why NOT To.* I have written this message to you from my heart, and there's a saying: "What leaves the heart, enters the heart." My hope is that it will enter into yours.

—David Sieff

SHACKING UP FROM A CHILD'S POINT OF VIEW

When you shack up with someone, are you aware of whom you're inviting into your home? Do you *really* know who that person is? What do your children think of them living with you? Can you really trust him or her with your children, especially when you're not around? These are just some of the very important questions you need to ask yourself before you invite someone to move in, especially when there are children involved. You never know what kind of element you are allowing into your home. You can truly damage your children (sometimes for life) if you permit someone to live with you that you don't know well and are not married to. What kind of example are you setting for your children?

Why not marry that person? If that person genuinely loves you, they would commit their life to you and marry you. They aren't looking for the easy way out because living together *is* the easy way out.

I asked many of these questions myself the first time my mother started shaking up. It actually brought a bad element into my home. On my tenth birthday, her shack-up honey and his friends decided that it would be fun to get me drunk. At ten years old, how do you think that affected me? Well, I can tell you that it wasn't a good or positive experience.

Another time, I remember when he and I went with his friend to the gas station. He came out with some alcohol. He told me that I had to drink all of what he had bought. So I started to, but I couldn't finish it—I was too full. He decided that since I hadn't finished it, he would put his cigarette out on my leg. How did that affect me as a child? I didn't understand it at all. I was scared—so scared of him that I never even told my mom. Did I do something wrong? I did what he said and he hurt me for it. I was just a child, it damaged me emotionally and psychologically to a degree. It can give kids thoughts of suicide, and it could ruin their self-esteem, making them think that they aren't good enough later in life. You never know just how much damage a child receives in circumstances like that.

Think about what you are doing before you decide to invite that person into your home. You not only invite *them* in, you invite a whole host of other things—like all their immoral habits *and* their immoral friends.

Consider your children's feelings before making that decision. Think about the things that could happen to them that you will never know about because they're too afraid to tell you. You could be allowing damage to be done to them and in turn they will take it into life with them.

There are many other events that happened to me with her shack-up honey's friends. Those are just two incidents that stand out in my mind the most. If you love your children, don't shack up. Consider my experience in the matter. The only saving grace for me was my positive point of view and my happy-go-lucky personality. Not every child is as fortunate as I was. If you love your children, consider and respect their feelings in the matter of inviting a stranger into their home. Children have the right to say how they feel about who lives with them. You and your children should make important decisions like that as a family.

—Isaiah James

"Shacking up" is without merit. I have experienced its baseness firsthand. I am Anne's middle son, Jacob.

There has been a lack of integrity with people in today's world. Most people don't care how they are seen by others, and when they place more value on desire than on worth of character, they have allowed degradation to their integrity and have permitted their credibility to be taken from them.

Whenever people asked me whether my mother had married again, I was always reluctant to tell them that she was living with her "boyfriend." It was shameful to me that she would live with someone without being married to him. There was more commitment on my mother's part than there was on his. My mother deserved better than what she got. But for my mother, it was difficult to withdraw from the situation she was in: She was taken with love and she couldn't imagine being without that person.

In this day, people *do*...then they *think.* They seldom recognize that their actions affect others. Don't jump into bed or move in just because the person you love *says* they love you, do it when they have already proven their intentions by marrying you. Don't go through all the painful nights that my mother went through. Think twice before "shacking up."

—Jacob James

FREQUENTLY ASKED QUESTIONS ABOUT
SHACKING UP

Question: *I feel I have high self-esteem and I'm living with my boyfriend; is it still a bad thing to do?*

Answer: Yes, it's bad to do! You think you have high self-esteem? Do you know what self-esteem means? Here's the definition: *"Belief in oneself, undue pride in oneself, conceit."* I think we all need to start looking up words more often so we don't use them out of context! Did you know what self-esteem meant? I didn't know exactly what it meant, until I looked it up. Now, let's remember what the definition for self-respect is: *"Having the proper respect for the DIGNITY of one's character."* If you had self-respect (not self-esteem), you wouldn't choose that lifestyle for the simple reason that you have dignity for your character.

I can't help but think about every woman that I've talked to about shacking up with her boyfriend...there's always some indication that they feel ashamed of it. I pay close attention to their body language, and their face, and it gives away what they really feel *every time*. For instance, when we talk about their arrangement, I see this: the head goes down or they will immediately look away...it almost always happens. That's the first indication that they feel ashamed. The next one is that they start talking a lot about why it's really okay! Look, what you really think about what you're doing reveals itself, and you don't even realize it—*but I do!*

197

You are deluding yourself if you think that you have high self-esteem. The very fact that you would lower your standards and live with a man before marriage *proves* that you don't care about yourself enough. You may do well in your trade, thus making you *feel* that you have high self-esteem, but that is in your professional life and has nothing to do with your personal life. Remember, your man knows that you don't respect yourself when you shack up with him, and let me remind you that he loves the fact that you think it's okay!! We have given men permission to use us…that is to our own undoing.

Question: *I really feel that I should live with my boyfriend first before we get married so I can "get to know him." What do you think about that?*

Answer: Ha, ha…You are kidding, right?! My husband likes to call this one the, "I have to get to know you" syndrome! First, let me say this to you: you never completely "get to know" someone in the time you're with them. Whether it's nine months or forty years, you'll always be "getting to know" that person, and you'll always see things you greatly dislike or even loath. That's the gamble you take when you decide to make a commitment of marriage; you just stick it out. It takes a lifetime to see things you don't like about that person…the question is then, are you woman or man enough to go the long haul? That's really the bottom line. Like I've said before, it's a little word called *maturity*.

When you shack up so you can "get to know" the person, you're already doing it for all the wrong reasons. You're already looking for all the negative in the relationship, so it's really doomed from the get-go.

Question: *This is a new millennium; shouldn't we just change with it?*

Answer: As I told Danny Bonaducci on the show "The Other Half," it doesn't mean it's a good millennium. And whether we women like it or not, this one fact will not change: for us, when we shack up with a man, we are still considered slutty for doing it. When a man shacks up with a woman he looks like a stud. We hold the gift of giving life in our hands—we give life or take it away. I believe that we have an awesome power that we haven't even yet understood.

Women who shack up don't care for themselves. The women I know who will not accept anything but a marriage proposal honor themselves *and* their bodies. Do yourself a favor, start honoring yourself because no one is going to do it for you. Demand the best for yourself, take nothing less than the best, and you'll attract a man that will love you for it. Believe me, men know a weak woman. Don't be one of them!

Question: *I have always considered myself a person with good, sound standards, and I have been with my boyfriend for 10 years. Even after this long, do you still think that it's wrong to do?*

Answer: You see the word "standard" that you wrote there? I've done you a favor; I've looked up the word so that you can see that you're basically deluding yourself about your "standard" of shacking up verses being married.

Here's the definition for standard: *"A level of excellence, attainment regarded as a measure of adequacy."* Now let's really think about this clearly. Let the definitions speak for your lifestyle and forget my opinion for a moment. Do you think shacking up is a level of excellence that you're living? Do you know what excellence means? (I'm learning, too, as I go along here, and I'm looking up the words as I'm writing.) Excellence means the following: *"The fact or condition of excelling, superiority surpassing goodness and merit."*

Wow! Come on, you can't read that and not be affected by its power. So, do you still think it's a good standard? I say that the answer is pretty self-explanatory, and it's time to leave him or get married. What do you say?

I need to add that since I've started looking up words and getting exact definitions, it has really helped paint a very clear picture—not to mention that it jars your senses and makes you much more conscientious of what you're doing and what kind of value it has to it. For instance, if you're hanging around a crowd that does drugs and steals, obviously it goes without saying that this is a low standard— they simply have no conscience. I'm sure you would agree with that. So, if we can measure the way we act and live by certain standards, then we would have to say that living together without being married is a low standard.

Let's look up the word moral...now let's see here...okay, here's the definition: *"Relating to or dealing with or capable of making the distinction between right and wrong in conduct."* BINGO! We have to have a set of standards or we would just be robots walking around. In order to know right and wrong, we have to see both sides and decide which path we will take, high ground or low. Think before you shack up. Really, the only person benefiting from it is your man...and he's really not yours if he doesn't want to marry you!

Question: *It's just a piece of paper...I don't need a piece of paper to give me permission to sleep with my boyfriend. What's your thought on that?*

Answer: That's a great point! "It's just a piece of paper!" If it's just a "piece of paper" there should be no problem in getting married! The truth of the matter is, *that* piece of paper *does* mean something! Like Rabbi Boteach says in his book *Kosher Sex,* "...although a symbol might indeed be construed as a mere two dimensional representation, our willingness to embrace or reject that symbol is, in fact, the weather vane for what we *feel* toward the object it represents." That is a brilliant statement!

One more thing, ladies; the Rabbi has this to say as well: "When a man wears a wedding ring, it is a statement to the outside world that not only is he in love with someone, but that he is proud of his commitment...so proud is he that he firmly and daily announces to the world that he belongs to someone!" Thank you, Rabbi. Coming from a man, that means a lot!

So, getting married means that you will be true to one person, that you will love and cherish that person, and that you will stick it out through thick and thin. The problem is that most people want an easy out. That's why shacking up is so popular; no one wants to have to work at anything in the relationship. If it gets uncomfortable, you just leave and start a new one...that's so easy! But how many times will you do it before you realize that it doesn't work that way, and that you've sacrificed your dignity and self-worth for something with no value. Marriage is the place where you can grow and become a better person—if growing up and being more spiritual is what you want in life.

Question: *I'm divorced and have a child who really loves my new boyfriend; would it be a bad decision for him to move in?*

Answer: After reading all the questions and answers, I would think that you would know by now that it's bad for your child. I thought about how I could answer this question, and it came to me through my physical therapist's assistant.

She has a little four-year-old daughter and she's divorced. Her child loves her new boyfriend, but like she told me, "We don't act all lovey-dovey in front of her. We've been seeing each other for a year, and we're really good friends. I won't move in with anyone unless I'm married, it's really an inappropriate thing to do." She is the example that people should look at. I commend her for her moral stand and for the fact that she has the brains to know that shacking up would hurt her daughter's well being.

Printed in the United States
19213LVS00005B/157-162